Ignite Your Inner Fire

Embrace Passion and Purpose

Compiled By Kyra Schaefer

Copyright © 2023 As You Wish Publishing

All rights reserved.

ISBN: 978-1-951131-61-6

No portion of this book may be reproduced in any form without written permission from the publisher, As You Wish Publishing connect@asyouwishpublishing.com, except as permitted by U.S. copyright law.

Not a substitute for mental, emotional or physical medical advice. All author's opinions are their own. If you need help please seek out a medical professional for advice.

Contents

Fireflies: A Lightworker's Guide to Enlightenment	1
By Beth Eiglarsh	
Discovering Purpose: A Journey of Healing and Connection	21
By Rina Escalante	
Choosing Your Own Adventure	37
By Karen Gabler	
Decide Not to Decide	53
By Sarah Gabler	
Opportunity	67
By Rosanne Groover Norris	
Forever with You	81
By Donna Kiel	
Standing At The Cliff's Edge	97
By Becki Koon	

The Awakening of Purpose	113
By Pedram Owtad	
Embracing Failure and Discovering New Horizons	133
By Kyra Schaefer	
Be Like a Five-Year-Old	155
By YuSon Shin	
Living The Dream	171
By Janice Story	
The Journey We Call Life	187
By Chantalle Ullett	
Midlife Motivation: Relighting an Extinguished Fire	201
By Janet Zavala	

CHAPTER

Fireflies: A
Lightworker's Guide to
Enlightenment
By Beth Eiglarsh

Beth Eiglarsh, a self-proclaimed perpetual student, is grateful for the many facets of wisdom she has gained on her colorful journey. Her gift is to share her story, and help others embrace theirs.

Beth is a Neuro-Linguistics Programming Life Coach, an Energy Healer/Advanced Usui, Kundalini and Lightarian Reiki Master, a Holographic Memory Resolution Trauma Therapist, a Spiritual Teacher and a gifted Intuitive. After years of success in advertising, followed by global recognition for her gift company, Beth fell into a downward spiral of chaos, chronic pain and workaholism. After intense introspective work and a radical pivot, Beth created a System for Living, called A.R.M.S. to help others navigate their journeys with greater ease and grace. She enjoys walking groups and individuals through her 4-step formula for raising Awareness, Remembering who you are, Manifesting your desires, and being of Service to self and others. Beth's system is explained in her book, *Beth's Case Scenario*, where she offers experiential learning through exercises and case studies.

Beth's greatest passion comes from helping people feel better, by empowering them to step into the most authentic version of themselves. She enjoys a balance of work and play, and loves spending quality time with her wonderful husband, three beautiful children, and Goldendoodle named Peace.

An "International Best-Selling Author," Beth penned *Beth's Case Scenario,* and contributed to *Enduring Wisdom, Whispers From The Heart,* and *Own Your Awesome.* She offers one-on-one sessions, A.R.M.S. workshops, and Mind, Body, Spirit retreats. For more information, go to www.SpeakToBeth.com

Chapter 1

Fireflies: A Lightworker's Guide to Enlightenment

By Beth Eiglarsh

Fire•fly (n) Soft-bodied beetle related to the glow-worm, with luminescent organs. The light is chiefly produced as a means of communication.

See also (n) The Firefly represents beauty, spirituality, inspiration, and idea. Its message is, "Your inner awareness is your guiding light." In our lives, a Firefly can become a symbol of light that leads every man to the homeland, and to a life that is complete.

See also (n) Lightworker

When I was a little girl growing up in Seneca, South Carolina, I was in awe of the little lights swirling in my wooded backyard. Drawn to the beauty, the wonder, and the light, my neighbor and I would catch fireflies and hold them hostage under a glow-in-the-dark frisbee. Worse, I would remove their light and use the "bulb" as a crayon to create a glowing masterpiece on my body. I feel terrible about the discomfort I caused those beautiful creatures. I wanted to shine like they did. Seeing "B E T H" illuminated on my forearm was the beginning of my life as a lightworker.

A lightworker is someone who feels an innate and undeniable pull to help others—to be a beacon, on a quest to neutralize negative energy and bring harmony to humanity. Similar to the firefly, lightworkers rise above worldly chaos to shine their light on the paths of those still in the dark. Both light beings bring hope as they quietly emanate their internal guidance system beyond their physical bodies, initiating availability.

Lightworkers carry out this mission in unique ways, gravitating towards spiritual professions such as caregiver, healer, bodyworker, or coach. Our essence, a.k.a. higher self, dictates our capability. Many don't awaken to their truth until they go through a transformational journey of self-discovery. Similar to a butterfly starting life as a caterpillar, the process requires a stint in murky darkness before awakening to a set of wings. Others find contentment in their role of that friend who others flock to for advice, one who holds a non-judgmental, loving space for retreat. Even those flightless fireflies with shortened or no wings use their light as a love language that articulates safety for those in need. Remembering that you are a guiding light is where the magic and the responsibility begin.

"The two most important days in your life are the day you are born and the day you find out why." —Mark Twain

My journey as a lightworker began with me flying freely in my adolescent years, averting obstacles in my teenage years, experiencing darkness in my 40s, and ultimately dying a spiritual death to reclaim my light and soar again.

Fireflies symbolize physical beauty and also transformational power where death leads to rebirth. My metamorphosis awakened me from my amnesia. I emerged as my authentic self. My experience turned to wisdom, my pain turned to empathy, and my self-actualization became the key to freeing others from their emotional life sentences.

Healing Without Boundaries

Like all beings, fireflies face numerous challenges, including pollution, habitat loss, pesticides, and climate change. With their population dwindling, they instinctively know to ward off predators with their unique chemistry. When threatened, they release a bitter chemical. Even with this system in place, some frogs consume them in such volume that they begin to glow.

I was 41 years old and the pain in my legs was so debilitating I could barely walk without pain medication. My physical ailments escalated to multiple diagnoses, including SI joint dysfunction, thoracic outlet syndrome, hip bursitis, public symphysis dysfunction, adrenal fatigue, oxidative stress, and "inexplicable leg pain." I sought neurologists, rheumatologists, acupuncturists, chiropractors, massage therapists, physical therapists, and psychotherapists.

My emotional distress led to chaos, confusion, anxiety, and exhaustion. My life had snowballed into an unmanageable blur. But how? I had nurturing parents, great friends, and enjoyable moments. I won awards, held leadership positions, married a wonderful man, built a beautiful family, and started my own company that went global. I was the picture of success.

Why couldn't I get out of bed?

Why was the pain so unbearable?

We are presented with what we need for our soul's growth; my pain led me to the root cause.

One day during a massage, my therapist speculated that I was an empath. When I asked her what that was, she began describing me. It resonated on such a deep level that I began to cry. I was an empath! I was an extra porous sponge who had energetically absorbed decades of other people's challenges, emotional imbalances, and physical limitations. I was a firefly, oblivious to her superpower. I was healing others without boundaries.

I called my Aunt Greta from the parking lot. She was a psychic, healer, and conduit to life beyond our galaxy. She was the obvious choice to share my news with. Through tears, I exclaimed, "I know what I am!" Without hesitation, she responded, "I've been waiting a long time for this call." Relief washed over me. The mystery of my physical depletion and mental overwhelm was found. I traded my fear for curiosity and replaced my guilt with compassion, understanding, and grace.

How would I navigate this new trajectory?

Greta continued. "A lot of people will want a lot of things from you. Be discerning with your energy." When you hold a lamp in the dark, people seek solace around you. Some borrow very little to illuminate their path. Others drain your battery until the light goes dim. Nobody is to blame. We are attracted to hope, inspiration, and shiny things. The glow of those fireflies in my backyard made them an easy target. My fascination and interference led to their slow death.

My revelation allowed me to pivot into a more rewarding and meaningful life. It also taught me that a boundary system was paramount for my health and well-being. Living a life of service had to start with me.

If you are reading this book, you are probably a lightworker. If the term "firefly" sparks an interest deep within your soul, I encourage you to burst out of your cocoon and into the most wonderous version of you! These two steps will guide you.

1.Charge your bulb.

2.Shine your light!

The order of this formula is as important as the formula itself. If lightwork does not come from an overflow of self-care, you are at risk for imbalance, resentment, and burnout. When your bulb is charged, you will organically look to fulfill your calling.

Step 1: Charge Your Bulb

Self-Care

The firefly emits light without losing heat. While their lights are off, they can be found on moist ground, hiding between tall blades of grass. Their preservation is contingent upon their time of retreat. As lightworkers, there are times that require you to be unavailable and reserve mindful time to prevent a short circuit.

We are programmed to be selfless, and we can forget to carve out essential downtime for replenishment. Self-care is not selfish; it reinforces self-love, which is not only critical for our health; it also keeps our motives pure.

Rituals, like a mini-date with yourself, are effective reminders that you are worth the devoted time. Beginning the day with inactivities such as meditation, affirmations, or journaling, will stabilize your system and make you less likely to be affected by the uncertainties of the day. It doesn't take a trip to the mountain tops in Tibet to realign and refuel your tank. You are one intentional breath away from a reset. You and your self are engaged in the longest relationship you will ever have. By loving yourself—not only, but first—you maintain the number one spot on your to-do list.

Intuition

The firefly's light mechanism originates in its abdomen. As air rushes in, it gives off the familiar glow. Our gut is referred to as our "second brain"—the seat of intuition. With 85% of serotonin, the feel-good hormone, produced in our abdomens, it's imperative to maintain a healthy environment for your internal

GPS to run optimally. Eliminate brain fog by choosing high-vibrational solutions: healthy foods, supportive friends, and uplifting conditions.

When we ignore our instincts and act on impulse, our blockages amplify. As sensitives, energy can feel so overwhelming that we may reach for a quick fix through negative behavior. Positive intent has little patience when the urgency to ground is critical. Unhealthy habits such as mind-altering substances, gluttonous foods, and spewing excess energy onto others provide immediate relief, creating a false sense of gravity. By ensuring that your abdomen is a safe place to land, you minimize the need to crash. Your choices either fuel your growth or hinder it. It's important to choose wisely.

"The only way out is through, and the only way through is within." —Beth

The longer I do this work, the more sensitive I become. Sounds are louder, tastes are stronger, and lack of compassion is more disheartening. The subtle accumulation of sensations, if not cleared, can result in fear and fatigue. When life gets challenging, double up on your self-care! Nurture your light source. Clear the cobwebs, calibrate the wattage and upgrade the switchboard. Release what doesn't belong to you and allow your intuition to flow unencumbered.

Ignite Your Flame

Humans go through life on an external quest for internal peace. If only I had a different partner, another job, a nicer car, or recognition—then, I would be happy. The firefly teaches us to believe in the infinite flow of resources available to us. We have all that we need—energy, inspiration, illumination, and possibilit . The emotional state we seek originates from within. The light we pursue is self-illumination. The passion that drives our mission exists in our Sacral Chakra, the energy center for joy.

If lightwork is your purpose, what is it powered by? It's important not to blur the lines between work—even if it lights you up—and personal creativity. A depletion in the Sacral Chakra can rob you of enjoyment. Part of recharging your bulb is to identify things that excite you. With so many obligations, it's easy to neglect that deeper part of you that's curious, that wants to play, and that desires new ways to explore fulfillment.

Joy is your birthright! Honor that part of you that wants to sing, dance, paint, write, or perform. Sit with your hands clasped beneath your belly button where ideas are birthed and ask, "When I connect with myself deeply, I get excited about_____!" See what comes forth. Then go do it. Ignite that flame and shine from the inside out.

Exercises for Recharging Your Bulb

Morning Invocation – Instead of racing out the door ready to save the world with an untamed auric field, mindfully place your cape on and create a boundary—supercharged with stipulations.

Before getting out of bed, draw an imaginary circle on the floor. Step into this circle and create a bubble of light around you. Create a statement to reinforce your needs. Example: "I will only allow exchanges for the highest good to penetrate my protective bubble today." Your words of intention carry a frequency to safeguard your energy. Say them aloud.

Invocation:

Waterfall Release – Instead of accumulating other people's energy and allowing it to snowball, implement a virtual cascade to assist in the releasing process. Use this tool when needed; between clients, after watching the news, following an unpleasant conversation, or after a lunch when your friend unloaded their challenges. Water dilutes intensity by cooling off, and permits what doesn't belong to you to float away. Add a verbal unambiguous statement of support. Example: "I let go of _____'s energy and all that it required of me, consciously, subconsciously, spiritually, physically, and emotionally."

Step 2: Shine Your Light

Be of Service To Others

Once you feel grounded and glowing, get outside of your head and step into someone else's world. The subtle shift to "How can I be of service at this moment?" allows you to come from an elevated place, with a firefly's view.

But what do I have to offer?

A lightworker's humility can be disguised as imposter syndrome. Do I know enough? Do I have what it takes? Am I enough? While you are capable of helping others even when harboring your own unhealed wounds, the joy of helpfulness offers a wonderful incentive to become a clear conduit. Shining at full capacity can be achieved by suspending your personal challenges. Your presence can provide the medicine for another's dis-ease. It could be a prescription for you too.

Get Vulnerable

Humanizing yourself is the purist form of service. After enduring a challenge, you hold a unique gift. Offering comfort to someone struggling on their journey can bring new meaning to yours. People crave being seen, heard, and understood. Your vulnerability provides a connection that whispers, "You are not alone." Your story is the catalyst that initiates a perspective shift that inspires strength and optimism.

Identify a life-changing situation that you suffered, such as illness, divorce, death, or depression. Connect with an individual or an organization that can benefit from your experience. Where can you offer your knowledge, strength and hope?

Some examples: Volunteer at a hospital, Google "support groups" and sign up to be a speaker, sponsor an addict, become a mentor, create a Facebook page where others can find a safe outlet, organize a food train for someone enduring cancer treatments, etc.

Stop playing it small! Take up space. Don't minimize your value because others have been doing this work longer. Your unique voice is necessary. The world needs your contribution. Sure, it's more comfortable to keep quiet and minimize your exposure. Our souls have incarnated to grow through earthly experiences and that requires getting uncomfortable. Look for ways to expand even if you're afraid. Confidence, value, and purpose are waiting for you on the other side.

Shine Your Unique Light

A client of mine survived a rare breast cancer. Prior to her diagnosis, she was the ultimate orchestrator of all her friend's events. She would forego sleep to create award-winning centerpieces, and trade self-care for the grateful smiles that arose from her thoughtfulness. Somewhere in the abyss of gut-wrenching fear, multiple surgeries, and forced downtime, a seed of promise was planted. She drew from her experience and founded an organization aimed to help others on similar journeys. Three annual galas later, she raised enough funds to assist countless people in seeking early detection. She re-ignited her flame by pouring her creative juices into intentional parties—with a purpose.

Look for ways to spread your love, by design, from that place within that sanctifies your oneness with creation and reminds you why you're here. Close your eyes and ask your soul where it wants to show up. Let your answer guide your next spirit-driven steps.

Exercises to Shine Your Light

Brighten Your Bulb – Breath is life, yet its mechanism is subconscious. Consciously use your breath to imitate a firefly and initiate availability. Be open to this illumination practice to attract new people, places, things, and situations that light you up.

Sit comfortably, close your eyes, and identify where in your body your seed of intuition is. Let that seed crack open to reveal a tiny bright light. With every inward breath, let that light grow bigger and brighter. With every exhalation, distribute the light within. Inhale until every cell, atom and molecule is radiating, then exhale that light in front and behind you, to the left and right of you, above and below you. Bask in this glow, while setting an intention to link to a person or situation that is ready for your enlightened message of hope and inspiration.

Random Acts of Kindness – An unexpected altruistic gesture brings joy to the giver and the receiver. Kindness is an expression of our truest nature. The possibilities are endless. When we activate our kindness, it beams us up to source energy where only love exists. Choose from the list below or create your own.

Pay the toll for the person behind you

Smile at a stranger

Ask a cashier how their day is going

Compliment someone on their appearance

Return your shopping cart

Bake cookies for your doctor and their staff

Tell a supervisor how good your service was

Donate blood

Tip the bathroom cleaning staff

Donate clothing to the homeless

Text a friend how special they are

Handwrite a love note

Carry a person's groceries to their car

Pay for extra time on someone's parking meter

Give an extra-long hug

Hold the door open for someone

Extend an unlikely invitation

Secretly pay another person's bill at a restaurant

Leave a friendly note on a stranger's car

Buy a co-worker coffee

Tip the drive-through worker

Leave a treat in the mailbox for your carrier

Surprise your spouse at the office

Support a friend's business

Help a disadvantaged child buy school supplies

Leave a positive review

Connect your Amazon account to a charity

Roll your neighbor's garbage bin off the street

Describe your experience

The Light At The End Of The Tunnel

Lightworker: "Get me off this planet!"

Same lightworker: "Waaaaait, I forgot I'm meant to be saving this place, raising the love frequency, and God knows what else." (Cue the laughter)

Lightwork is a sacred mission to wake the planet by raising awareness beyond human conditions. Don't let that inner voice that exclaims, "I'm human, too," stop you from tapping into your ultimate assignment. You are a brilliant soul doing universal work, and you are expanding in the process. Be easy on yourself. Embrace your journey adorned with the light of lampposts, fireworks, fluorescent bulbs, flames, eclipses, and shooting stars. Life is a beautiful light show. Wisdom dictates which lens you choose to see it through.

"What you seek is seeking you." —Rumi

Perhaps those fireflies in my backyard were seeking me. Their light sparked my inner flame, which prompted my soul's quest.

How can you shine your light?

How can you help others find theirs?

CHAPTER

Discovering Purpose: A Journey of Healing and Connection
By Rina Escalante

Rina Escalante is a first-generation Salvadorian-American from the Mission District of San Francisco. She raised two daughters on her own after she divorced their father when they were 3 ½ and 1 ½ and now they are both mothers. She has five grandchildren ranging in ages from 17 to nine.

She used to work in Corporate America but was sidelined due to life-altering strokes, where she had to relearn how to do practically everything, including relearning how to speak both her languages, Spanish and English, and was left legally blind after her second stroke. She is also a cancer survivor, being diagnosed with Papillary Carcinoma in 2017 that had spread, but she thrives! After a decade of rehabilitation

BY RINA ESCALANTE

from her ailments, she attempted to work again at Vail Resorts, in South Lake Tahoe at Heavenly Ski Resort winning Epic Service Awards three years in a row, but after catching Covid for the third time, it affected her detrimentally since she already had a compromised immune system. She left feeling distressed, knowing there are still people that think Covid is not real and do not take safety precautions to respect others.

Rina uses writing as a form of occupational and emotional therapy, hoping her stories help others besides herself.

She may be contacted at rinaesca@gmail.com

Chapter 2

Discovering Purpose: A Journey of Healing and Connection

By Rina Escalante

"The Creator is not going to ask me how much did you accumulate? He's going to ask me, did you put the gifts I gave you to good use?" —Dr. Clarissa Pinkola Estes

A profound sense of purpose has burned within me, igniting my soul and guiding my path like a power source from my earliest memories. It has been the only true fire I have ever known, my constant and most dependable companion; it has been and continues to be a journey of learning to trust her guidance. I was raised devoutly Catholic and sought understanding from the nuns who surrounded me like blue angels. Although I was unable to express the premonitions, feelings, and gifts that flowed freely through me like automated power surges, it would have been impossible for them to comprehend the depth of my soul's calling; deep in my heart, I remained steadfast in my unwavering conviction. I am going to bring you along on my poignant and transformative journey, chronicling my pursuit of self-discovery, healing, and connection. Through the intricate tapestry of life's challenges, the guidance of Spirit, the presence of angels, and the wisdom of my ancestors, I strive to fulfill my purpose and embrace a life of profound meaning I know I am meant to have and willingly share knowledge as part of my purpose. Devotion and openness to endure growing pains are necessary as part of the life journey. I am discovering and learning to embrace this practice of growth, expansion, and exploration for the greater good of myself and the future of my descendants.

The Unexplainable Flame Within:

From the tender age of innocence to the complexities of adulthood, I have carried this burning light within me in the depths of my being. As I dove into my awakening, I was exposed to the seven main chakras and initially attributed this flame to their intricate energy centers attempting to gain a deeper understanding of self. As I ventured deeper into holistic understanding, I was able to unearth its true nature—a truly divine fire, an indelible mark of the eternal within me. This flame has been my constant companion, urging me to persevere through life's trials, offering solace in times of doubt, and reminding me of the presence of a higher power, gently guiding my steps and ensuring I never felt truly alone, even during my lowest moments. This higher power, divine love, has always given me the greatest gift, that of hope, something we all need to continuously forge on. The reassurance I could always depend on, the familiar fire in the center of my being as a signal of either a warning of impending danger or of confirmation.

The Angels Among Us:

Throughout my journey, I have been profoundly blessed to continuously intersect with remarkable souls who have graced my path—beings that I can only lovingly refer to as angels. These angels, manifested in human form or ethereal beings, appeared at precise moments when I needed them or we needed each other the most. Their loving support, unwavering encouragement, and selfless acts of kindness have surprisingly reaffirmed my faith in the inherent goodness of humanity. Through their presence, I have learned to trust the divinity that resides within me, even when faced with the fallibility of human nature.

My Healing Journey:

In recent years, I have chosen to embark on an awe-inspiring journey of healing and self-discovery, delving into the depths of my past lives through the profound practice of hypnotherapy and embracing various modalities of holistic healing, including Reiki. Through this arduous yet transformative process, I have learned and accepted significant aspects of my purpose to break generational cycles of ancestral trauma and feel the work I am doing at this exact moment makes it meaningful. I sense the benefit will be for future generations. Embarking on my path of healing—physically, emotionally, and spiritually—I hope to liberate future generations from the shackles of these deeply ingrained and unhealthy patterns, ushering in a legacy of resilience, wholeness, and liberation from chains of unhealthy existence and transition to healthy stress-free lives.

During this transformative process, I questioned my resolve and my worthiness, asking myself, "Can I do this? Do I have the strength in me?" Conflicted within my soul, it is a necessary part of growth, asking whether I wanted to continue with my journey of discovery. Guided by the divine, my ancestors, and angels, self-investment work requires unyielding and undisturbed effort. There have been many times during my transformative journey when I have felt handcuffed, unable to move or grow due to a multitude of reasons. Accepting insecurities and imperfections and having the willingness to be open and learn are needed and desired so the luminous within may be free to guide me to a transformative legacy. With each chapter of life, I discover more of myself and what is compelling my spirit force.

Placing gates around myself is a tactic I use for self-preservation. The types of gates I use are: spiritual, protective, and ethereal. I use these gates for guidance and protection. I feel it necessary to protect my divinity because once I chose to be different, I became an outsider. As if it is a choice. As it relates to religion, the scrutiny is worse. I can no longer deny who I am to make others feel comfortable. I cannot push down my gifts, ignore they exist, or turn my back on my divinity. If I must stand alone, I will. I will not let family members control my narrative because they do not "believe in" who I am.

I have a burning desire to be a healer. It is necessary to heal myself so I can transform and become the healer the divine guides me to become. After a decade of complex medical complications, I have worked on my recovery daily since that fateful day in 2010, and fine-tuning my abilities has become part of my daily practice. My emotional well-being will be my final attainment to complete my healing so I may become a practicing practitioner, which is my end goal. But at this moment, it is unattainable because I am not yet wholly healed, and neither is my family. Nurturing is not only something we do to babies and children but something imperative to impart to ourselves daily. I count, am worthy, and I love myself. I must impart this healing work upon myself to set an example for future generations. We will all grow together and help each other to heal and be part of the greater good for all.

Living in Gratefulness:

I am grateful I was taught certain practices and rituals and learned how to be a faith-centered person in my Catholic school. I have discovered that regardless of how the divine has guided me to practice my spirituality presently, old habits die hard, even when I work towards the expansion of my spirit. I still hold on to my Saint cards and am unable to fall asleep without reviewing my day to ensure I can be a better person, praying, and upon waking, saying out loud that I am grateful I woke up to look down and see the daisies not look up to see them. These reflective thoughts, reviews, and prayers vacillate between Spanish and English. I am fundamentally unable to speak to Spirit in one language, and I find that my guides, ancestors, and the divine speak to me in what is most natural to my bilingual mind. I am aware of who is speaking to me based on the language they are speaking and by the sound of their voices, even the ancestors I have never met, which is quite interesting. I know who is speaking to me. Such a blessed gift from the Creator; how could I not live in gratefulness? This gift works in partnership with the channeling that comes through with my line-of-sight gift. I know this is attributed to the flame that has always burned within me, I have no doubt. I have always been devout and have not deviated from my faith in knowing there is a greater power in charge of it all. Free will is a gift I use to control my decisions and the path I choose to take, which means the lessons are also mine to own. The "line of sight" or "gift of sight" means I can see the choices before me, like scenes in a movie.

As I continue to pursue my holistic learning, I feel the divine's guidance getting stronger within me the more I seek. I have a deep-rooted burning desire within for knowledge to continue to regain the gifts my spirit was born with, and I will continue on my path to elevate my spiritual awareness as it is a passion within me I must quench. This fire has been the purpose I have always been seeking. I know there has to be a reason why I have been given these gifts that I shut off as a young mother.

Connecting with Spirit:

During the solitude imposed by the unprecedented global pandemic, I found myself delving even deeper into introspection, reclaiming the forgotten facets of my being, and reigniting the dormant flames of my soul. Through an overwhelming multitude of spiritual courses, dedicated inner work, and rehabilitative practices to heal and nurture my mind, body, and spirit, I began to forge a profound connection with Spirit and reignite gifts I was unable to manage in my late 20s early 30s when I was desperately searching for a spiritual mother. I was unsuccessful in finding her. I felt lost and thought my only choice was to "turn off" the gifts given to me by spirit. I do not know how I did it back then, but I once again feel the pure love of Spirit and feel secure enough to reopen myself to receive messages and accept guidance from my ever-present spirit guides, angels, and ancestors. As a young mother, I did not feel in control of the seemingly endless gifts I was given. Channeled messages from the other side flowed out of my mouth, and they did not end until the message was delivered to the intended group or individual. These channeled messages made me feel like an orator for the divine. I had no control over what was being said. My physical body was just a shell. I would feel as if the spirit of someone passed had entered my body to deliver a "message in time." I received other downloaded messages through my guides to my soul, people's past lives and their relationships with each other. I also intuitively knew how to do readings with tarot cards, which is something my Catholic family would have never exposed me to. It is now almost thirty years later, and due to all the expansive teachings I have immersed myself in, I have learned how to ground properly for the work my soul does. I begin by placing my feet firmly on the ground about one foot apart, and I spread my toes. I take three large, clearing breaths using my arms and open hands to help clear out stagnant energy. I tap deep into mother earth and far into father sky, using my index finger as a guide through each step. Next, I surround myself with protection from my four main Archangels that identified themselves to me during my internship courses, and the League of 100,000 Angels surround me next. I tap into the sacred grid using my open hands as guides to tap in. I surround myself with my ancestors for guidance like a cloak and work in partnership with my spirit realm, including specific angels that I work with, which I bring in using my left hand, and close by bringing in Spirit's White Light of Purity and Protection. I know I am successful in 'tapping in' the moment I can feel a pulse of pure energy flow through me, and I feel powerful, protected, and at peace. I imagine this feeling is similar to plugging into a wall socket, as we can see how the energy flows once we flip a switch. This powerful flow of strength, power, and essence of protection is what I was missing as a young woman. The energy flow I feel has refamiliarized my divination skills. I work with copious divination tools, and interpretation of signs that I see and hear everywhere, and I notice more synchronicities. My intuition has deepened, empowering me to allow the inner compass that leads me toward my purpose with faith and hopes for my future. In the past, I doubted my inner sense and my instinct, and I now feel secure trusting my abilities and knowing how to protect myself and how to say no to my guides when there is information I am not comfortable seeing or relaying. It was this specific reason I turned off my gifts so long ago. I was seeing things about people I did not want to know, and I did not know how to stop seeing them. I was very frightened because the things I was seeing had to do with the ugliness of life and death.

Gratefulness Practice:

I was taught to live in gratefulness and I exhibit this practice through my evening and morning rituals which I cannot function without. When I began my awakening journey, I was taught to formalize this practice by starting a gratitude journal, and it has evolved into an evening gratitude practice. It has brought me great joy, peace, and continued growth, and I can see and feel the positive, energetic shift it has brought into my life force. Energy surrounds us, be it positive, negative, or neutral. Energy can be found everywhere and surrounds everything. I have discovered on some days, I only need gratitude grounding. On other days I am sent on astral travels, and this particular day I am going to share, Spirit decided I was ready to see again. As I sit here and write these words, I am once again receiving confirmation: my hair is standing on end, I have goosebumps running down my legs, across my body and my eyes are filled with uncontrollable emotion. My ancestor (Tia Elvy) is speaking to me at this moment, in Spanish of course, "Mi Nena, es necesario separarse de el veneno." My girl, it's necessary to separate yourself from the poison. "It's necessary for growth," she keeps repeating to me.

End of transmission.

That is her message and possibly that is the message she wants to relay to anyone who reads this piece. La paz con usted she sends. Peace be with you.

I told you, confirmation it just happens and I have no control.

Before beginning my practice:

I find a comfortable spot to sit undisturbed. With my eyes closed, I clear all energy from the day so I can have a conversation with the divine by taking three huge clearing breaths. I use my arms and open hands in a pushing motion to guide the air out of my body. By the third breath, my body is usually ready. On this specific day of practice, I was transcending into my gratitude trance. I let out my third huge breath, releasing my heart-centered essence. I began to feel that burning flame deep inside my soul, burning like a furnace; I knew something was happening. I began to see again! Scenes began flashing in front of me like little movie clips and then words streamed through in a straight line "Gift of Sight." Then all of a sudden, I saw my right hand moving up and down, with only two fingers extended as if saying "move along," but the message was very clear that I was regifted premonition, my very first gift from the divine! As soon as the scenes ended, my eyes popped open. When this happens, it is a sign that I have completed either meditation, trance, or astral travel. I am so grateful! I am no longer afraid of what I may see. I am prepared because I now have the guidance, light, and passion to serve. This experience gives me hope that other gifts, like the ability to see auras, will return. I am here for it.

Lessons from Life's Adversities:

Life, with all its intricate twists and turns, has presented me with a multitude of challenges that have tested my resolve and veered me away from the path illuminated by my inner flame. Faced with fear, societal stigmas, and the remnants of past traumas, I have sometimes faltered and questioned the validity of my purpose. However, in each adversity lies an opportunity for growth and transformation. With unwavering determination and the support of those that choose to walk this constantly evolving journey with me, I have learned to navigate the stormy seas of doubt, emerging more resilient and deeply connected to the essence of purpose within my soul.

As I reflect upon my journey of healing, connections, and self-discovery, I feel worthy knowing that I am open to growing, learning, and realizing that purpose is not a static destination but a dynamic force that continuously unfolds, revealing new layers of understanding and opportunities for constant expansion. Evolution and expansion are what my soul requires. My journey is an ever-evolving dance between self, and the universe, establishing regular connections with Mother Earth, renewing relationships with my ancestors who guide me, intimate conversations with the divine, and a call to live a life of meaning and impact. In embracing my purpose, I have discovered that it extends beyond my fulfillment, reaching out to touch the lives of others, the most important impact left for my descendants, and inspiring them to embark on their transformative journeys of healing, connection, and self-discovery. With a heart overflowing with gratitude, I step forward, guided by the flames of purpose, ready to embrace the limitless possibilities that await me.

CHAPTER

Choosing Your Own
Adventure
By Karen Gabler

Karen Gabler is an award-winning attorney, intuitive mentor, psychic medium, animal communicator and Reiki master. She also is a best-selling author, teacher and inspirational speaker. Karen is passionate about encouraging others to find their highest purpose and live their best lives. She mentors her clients through a variety of personal and business issues, marrying her practical legal and business experience with her innate intuitive ability to receive information and guidance from higher sources. She also facilitates connections with clients' loved ones in spirit. Karen conducts workshops and presentations on a variety of business, spiritual and personal development topics. She earned her

Bachelor of Science in Psychology from the University of Hawaii and her Juris Doctorate from the William S. Richardson School of Law at the University of Hawaii.

Karen has pursued wide-ranging education in interpersonal development and the spiritual sciences, working with tutors from the prestigious Arthur Findlay College for the Psychic Sciences in England as well as with numerous intuitives and mediums throughout the United States. She is a WCIT in the Martha Beck Wayfinder life coaching program. Karen enjoys reading, hiking, horseback riding and spending time with her husband and two children.

You can find Karen at www.karengabler.com

Chapter 3

Choosing Your Own Adventure

By Karen Gabler

By the time I was in high school, my future as an attorney was preordained. I wrote my first "legal memo" to my mother when I was a preteen, arguing about why I should be allowed to keep all of the record albums in my room instead of letting my older sister have any of them. I prided myself on citing clear evidence to prove that my little sister was hassling me instead of the other way around. I debated my parents on every topic and appealed every punishment. I took speech and theater classes, always presenting another argument or story to my audience.

At 21 years old, I entered law school and immersed myself in my studies. Instead of taking summers off, I accepted clerkships with local law firms, researching and writing case briefs. After graduation, I passed the Hawaii bar exam and accepted a legal associate position with one of Honolulu's largest law firms. As a junior attorney, I pulled all-nighters researching my clients' cases and then marched into court the following morning, energized by the power of youth and the anticipation of victory.

Thirty years later, the power of youth had dissipated and there were too many victories to count. I had built a thriving law practice, expanded my client base from a few hundred to several thousand companies, and won numerous awards for client service and professional acumen. By all accounts, I had achieved professional success. And yet, I could feel the fluttering of my heart and soul, wondering, "What else? Is this all there is? Isn't it time to see what else I can do?"

As these thoughts began to stir, I began to recognize that there was something else I wanted and needed to do. Ten years earlier, I had seen internationally-known psychic medium John Edward doing audience readings on television. I wanted to feel my own departed loved ones around me, so I attended a workshop intended to help attendees develop their own psychic medium abilities. As a lawyer focused on evidence and logic, I had no expectation that I was a medium myself, but I was stunned to find that I was capable of picking up energetic information that I could not possibly have known while doing practice readings for my fellow workshop participants. The instructor assured me that I was indeed a medium and encouraged me to pursue my gifts.

That initial workshop turned into hundreds of hours of psychic medium development courses and mentorships with numerous national and international tutors over the next decade. My spiritual work expanded as I learned how to master my gifts. I was enthralled with every spiritual connection and emotionally overwhelmed as healing messages came through for my recipients. I realized that I was incredibly passionate about making these intuitive connections, and became increasingly frustrated with the heavy demands of my law practice that took me away from my spiritual work.

Searching for validation of my growing dissatisfaction, I suggested to friends and colleagues that I wanted to more fully explore my spiritual work and might take a step back from my legal career. I received the same reaction repeatedly: "What? But you are so good at being a lawyer, and you are so successful! Why would you want to do anything else?" I explained that it was challenging to speak to unhappy people all day; no one calls an attorney merely to confirm that all is well in their world. I reminded people that I had been an attorney for over thirty years and wanted to explore other options. I asserted that I was passionate about my psychic medium activities and felt uplifted whenever I worked with intuitive energy. Those around me continued to question my judgment. "But why would you throw away a career after working so hard for it? Why would you give up all that effort you've put in? Your clients need you!"

It's fulfilling to be accomplished in your career, but being good at something doesn't mean it drives us, nor does it mean we should do it forever. We often pursue activities out of loyalty to others, pressure from those from whom we seek approval, or fear of being labeled a quitter. We may struggle to determine what inspires us, or feel stymied by the demands of day-to-day life. We may be fearful of making a significant leap, wondering if there will be a net below to catch us. Despite these very human obstacles, when we allow ourselves to fully pursue our soul's purpose, we have the opportunity to live the life of vibrance that is truly intended for us.

What if you don't know how to find your passion?

You are in good company; most people don't know how to pinpoint their passions and may fear that they never will. There are a number of ways that you can begin to uncover the things that drive you on a soul level.

First, try making a list of things you love to do. No idea is too silly or unrealistic; include everything that crosses your mind, no matter how outlandish it may seem.

If you think to yourself, "I don't do anything outside of work," or "I have no idea what I love," consider the small moments in life where your interests may reveal themselves if you give them space to do so. What captures your attention when you are scrolling the Internet? What do you like to watch on television? What topics fill your conversations? Think back to your childhood: what did you most enjoy? What did you pretend to be when you let your imagination run wild? What did you love that you haven't done for years? What did you dream of doing that you haven't let yourself consider?

Another option is to ask your friends and family to share their observations with you. Those closest to us often are more aware of our gifts than we are, and appreciate them more than we do. They see the ideas and activities that inspire us, and they recognize the light in our eyes when we are acting from the heart. In using this approach, it is important to weed out commentary from those who are speaking from a place of fear: if someone close to you rejects the idea of stepping out of your comfort zone, they may be projecting their own hesitations and limitations onto you. Look for input from those who truly have your best interests at heart and want you to shine no matter how it impacts or frightens them.

What if you just don't recognize a feeling of passion toward anything in particular? We may be asking too much of ourselves if we insist that our passion must knock us off our feet. One of the best ways to feel the stirring of passion within you is to make space for intrigue and possibility. We often become so entrenched in our usual activities that there's no room for something unique in our lives. Shake up your patterns and let yourself wonder, "What's next?" You can start with something as simple as trying a new food for breakfast or taking a different path to your local grocery store. Small steps can begin to open your mind to options, which can lead to trying a new activity or finding a new source of joy.

What about the voice in your head that says, "That's not realistic. You can't do that! That's irresponsible!"? First, ask yourself whose voice is speaking to you in those moments. Is it a parent that told you it would be smarter to choose the secure career path? Is it a teacher who told you that you weren't good enough to pursue an area of interest? Ask yourself if the voice's admonitions are true. Is your dream really unrealistic? Why? And even if it is a bit unrealistic, does that mean that you shouldn't pursue it at all?

For example, imagine that your dream is to be an Olympic-level ice skater. Maybe it's not entirely realistic to expect that you can compete at Olympic levels in a sport you've never tried, against athletes who have spent their entire lives training for this moment. Does that mean that you can't take ice skating lessons at your local ice rink? Does it mean you can't enjoy a day of skating with friends? We are quick to assume that if following our passion isn't likely to lead us to a life-changing event, it isn't worth doing at all. This is a dangerous lie we tell ourselves, because it prevents us from exploring all the opportunities and options that might bring us joy, passion and vibrance in our lives. Why must we fully complete or succeed in everything we do? What if we just enjoy doing it regardless of skill or prospects, in the same manner that we enjoyed kicking a ball as a child without worrying about whether we would ultimately play World Cup soccer?

When I first began doing intuitive readings and coaching for clients, I worried about whether I would be "good enough." I wondered if I was truly ready to offer my services to others, and whether I would be a solid ambassador for the spirit world. I created tremendous angst for myself by judging my efforts before I even tried. As I worked to overcome my doubts, I realized that I was rapidly losing the joy in my spiritual work. It was becoming stressful and stilted as I picked apart and judged every reading. I finally realized that in setting extraordinary expectations for myself, I was forgetting the miracle of spirit communication and the wonder of connecting with others on a soul level. When I let go of the pressure to achieve and focused on the excitement and power of intuitive connections, I regained my joy and ignited my passion once again.

What if I can't afford to pursue my passion?

To bypass your human concerns and ignite your passions, think back to your childhood. When you woke up in the morning, did you consult a list of activities for the day that would promote your long-term goals? Did you wonder whether playing on the swings or drawing a picture would facilitate your career aspirations? Did you question whether buying a chocolate cone from the ice cream truck would derail your budget plan?

Granted, adults have greater responsibilities. We have bills to pay, decisions to make and tasks to perform. This doesn't mean that we can't leave room in our lives to explore our passions. We have been taught that living a passionate life would mean that we have been lucky enough to find a job or career aligned with our passion. While it would be nice to be paid for pursuing our passions, it is not a prerequisite to including those passions in our lives. There is nothing wrong with working in a job that supports your needs, while also pursuing your passions outside of your work.

As I began developing my mediumship and intuitive abilities, I spent almost a decade taking classes, participating in mentorships, and practicing my skills. At the same time, I knew that my spiritual work wasn't going to financially support my family in the same manner as my law career, particularly while I was caring for young children and elderly parents. I continued to diligently serve my law clients each week, fitting in my intuitive readings whenever possible. It was daunting and exhausting, but it was also exhilarating. As time moved on and my life circumstances progressed, I was able to devote a greater percentage of my time to my spiritual work while cutting back on my legal work.

Pursuing your passion doesn't mean you have to leap into the abyss and hope for the best. Find ways to carve out portions of your life to explore those activities and dreams that fill your heart. Even five minutes of passion pursuits each day will begin to infuse your life with a greater level of joy, and that joy feeds upon itself and continues to expand.

What if the thought of pursuing your passion terrifies you?

Quite frankly, pursuing your passion *should* terrify you. Why? Because it matters to you. Your day-to-day job—the one that merely pays your bills—isn't frightening, and it shouldn't be. It doesn't make your heart sing, so there's no risk in discovering that it's not really what drives you. It's the things that we know we were meant to do, the things that make us feel alive, the things that feed our soul, that hold the highest risk for us.

When the stakes are high, the fear can be intense, because we feel that we have so much to lose. As a practical matter, we could lose our income, our place on the corporate ladder, our reputation or our security. More importantly, we may feel like we've lost a piece of ourselves if we think that we have failed in pursuing our passions, or that we have failed to reach our highest potential in an area that means so much to us.

To avoid letting this fear become immobilizing, it is important to remember that our growth doesn't come from succeeding in our passions. Instead, it comes from *pursuing* them. Returning to our ice skating example, if you try ice skating but aren't able to reach your dream of becoming an Olympic-level ice skater, does that mean you have failed? Does that mean it was a mistake to try? Of course not. If you face your fears, put on a pair of skates and glide around the ring (and fall, and get back up again), you have opened the door to greatness on a soul level. You have allowed yourself to dream, and you have allowed yourself to try. If you spent ten minutes letting your heart feel free and your soul feel alive, you have won. The more you do this, the more success you have achieved. Our lives aren't measured by the accolades we've received or the money we've earned. The true measure of success is the extent to which we have lived, loved, laughed, attempted, created and explored, as we were meant to do.

As I pursued my spiritual work, I experienced tremendous self-doubt and fear of failure. At first, I wondered why I felt so panicked at the thought of making intuitive connections for others. After all, I was representing the spirit world, just as I represented my law clients. I was highly educated in my spiritual work, just as I had been in my legal work. Why didn't I feel as confident in my spiritual work as I did in my legal career? I realized that my fear stemmed from the knowledge that my spiritual work held great meaning for me. Providing accurate and meaningful messages to my spiritual clients is my passion and my soul's purpose. Eventually, I learned to channel my fear into the desire to serve with the utmost integrity and empathy, appreciating the miracle of spirit communication and the joy of connection.

Get comfortable with not knowing what comes next.

We typically feel more secure when we know what lies ahead. We make lists and manage calendars. Our society supports multi-million dollar annual sales of planners and organizational tools and supplies, helping us to feel in control of our lives. And yet, living the most vibrant life comes from remaining open to what may come, instead of limiting ourselves to our most mundane expectations.

While driving with my 16-year-old daughter and chatting about her upcoming senior year in high school, the topic turned to filling out her college applications and selecting a major that would promote her career interests. She said, "You know, what I really want to do in college is to remain completely open to what might come up for me. I want to try different things and explore options that I haven't really considered before." I was silent as I contemplated the unabashed freedom she had just expressed. "Does that worry you?" she asked. I took a deep breath and said, "Absolutely not, sweetheart. What I want for you—what I *truly* want for you—is for you to live your entire life in that manner. To be open to whatever comes your way. To try different things, and to explore your options. Please don't stop doing this after college. Please do this *forever*."

The greatest joy in life can be found by not knowing what will come next. Of course, this is not what we are taught, is it? Career coaches and guidance counselors offer a wide variety of psychological tests and skills assessments designed to tell us exactly what we should do, so that we can get on with the business of doing it. Those who are willing to go wherever the wind takes them are the exception to the rule. Instead of celebrating them, we tend to think of them as unmotivated, irresponsible, or lacking in direction.

In her 1997 column entitled "Advice, Like Youth, Probably Wasted on the Young" (immortalized in the "Wear Sunscreen" song remix by Baz Luhrmann), author Mary Schmich said, "Don't feel guilty if you don't know what you want to do with your life. The most interesting people I know didn't know at 22 what they wanted to do with their lives. Some of the most interesting 40-year-olds I know still don't."

It is never too late to explore your passions, and it is never too late to take your life in a new direction. What can you do to shake up your life today? What can you explore that would lift your energy and excite your heart? What steps can you take to let your soul take charge? Give your wings a chance, and you will soon take flight.

CHAPTER

Decide Not to Decide
By Sarah Gabler

Sarah Gabler is 17 years old and is a senior in high school. She loves playing games with her family and traveling to new places. Sarah enjoys playing the ukulele and guitar, singing and dancing, and riding her horse. As a lifelong artist, she loves using creative outlets to express her artistic vision. Sarah is an internationally best-selling author and has contributed her work to multiple published collections of short stories. She has been a stage manager for her high school productions, and loves bringing a show to life to entertain others. She hopes to study abroad during her college years and looks forward to exploring the world. Sarah is passionate about empowering people by helping them to recognize their true potential in the world, and plans to do motivational speaking in the future. Sarah began exploring spiritual teachings, self-development and soul empowerment concepts when she was 10 years old, and believes it has made her a better person today. It has motivated her to find ways to live her best life, and to help others on their journey to live their best lives as well. Sarah believes that even the smallest act of kindness can make someone's day, and she enjoys going out of her way to make others feel loved.

Chapter 4

Decide Not to Decide

By Sarah Gabler

"Life is about not knowing, having to change, taking the moment and making the best of it, without knowing what's going to happen next." —Gilda Radner

As a student currently in the first few months of my senior year of high school, I am preparing myself for a plethora of changes ahead of me and facing the pressure to choose a career to which I want to devote my life. Throughout my entire childhood, adults encouraged me to decide what I wanted to do for a career as soon as possible, always asking, "What do you want to be when you grow up?" This mindset, on top of being a child who has always had a hard time living in the present moment, caused me to be hyper-focused on my future "grand plans" and determine what I was going to do with my life. While it would seem handy to have a career path planned from the get-go, this caused me a lot of unnecessary stress. I have learned from my experiences that the best-case scenario often is not to know what you want to do next.

When I was little, I was obsessed with fashion design. I had hundreds of notebooks and sketchbooks filled to the brim with drawings and fabric samples of dresses and shirts that I wanted to make. I also constantly tried to make bags, jewelry, or hats that I designed. I adored going into clothing or fabric stores and feeling all the materials, trying on different shapes and sizes of clothes and getting new patterns and textures to play with and make into something new. Every single Christmas, I asked my parents for new fabrics, dress patterns, buttons, accent pieces (such as brooches or unique pins), and I even asked for and received a sewing machine. I also received a dress mannequin from one of my mom's coworkers. I was so excited to pursue a career in the field of sewing and fashion design.

For all of my elementary school and middle school years, fashion design was all I did and all I ever wanted to do. I never considered doing anything else even for a moment. Any time a college counselor or representative came to my school auditorium and mentioned that students should start thinking about what they might want to do as their careers or pathways, I would hold my head up high knowing that I already knew exactly what I was going to do with my life. I felt so ahead of the game, and incredibly secure in my future.

During eighth grade, while working on a class project regarding our long-term plans, I researched colleges that would offer the best opportunities for me in the field of fashion design. I presented on the history of fashion design and what I was planning to do with it in the future, stating that I was going to be taking classes in high school that would teach me more about fashion design, and would be attending FIDM (Fashion Institute of Design and Merchandising) in downtown Los Angeles for my college education. Perfect for staying close to family while pursuing my dreams! I continued with my presentation by explaining that after my schooling had finished, I would find a way to open a small store in California to start my own business and build my own clothing empire, all made and designed by me. I had my entire future planned out for myself. I made myself business cards, developed a website, and started social media accounts to begin making my dreams a reality. I knew exactly where I was going, I knew exactly how to get there, and I had no desire to do anything else with my life...or so I thought.

Despite all my ambition, toward the end of middle school, I felt that I had lost my spark for fashion design. I did not feel like sewing any longer. I was tired of sketching dresses and making the same old bags repeatedly. When I went to craft stores with my parents, I found myself feeling disinterested in the fabrics, and eventually found myself straying away from the fashion design aisles. I figured that this was just an "artist block" situation and didn't think much of it. Surely, I would regain my passion soon and be able to jump back into my plan.

Unfortunately, this did not happen. I waited for many months for my heart to rediscover its love for fashion design, but I was never able to find joy in the creative process of fashion again. I felt dread every time I thought about forcing myself to make something. This sudden shift in my attitude led me to feel completely lost and disoriented. I felt confused in myself and unfocused in my education. I was entering high school knowing that what I always thought I wanted to do no longer sparked passion or excitement in me. I was terrified that "the future" I had been preparing for my entire life was coming soon, and I had no clue what I wanted to do anymore.

I attended my ninth-grade high school orientation a few weeks after I realized that my perfect future was not going to work for me. I scanned through the registration sheet with all the classes that were available for me and desperately searched for something that would even slightly interest me while also feeling an immense amount of bitterness that I now had to rethink what I wanted to do with my life.

I finally decided to register for a collection of graphic design classes in my ninth and tenth grades that consisted of learning all the ins and outs of Adobe software and how to make product packaging more noticeable and pleasing to the eye. I found these classes quite fascinating, but I remained frustrated while attending my class periods because I wasn't filled with the same passion that I had for fashion design in prior years. However, I was desperately trying to find a new passion that would stick, so I continued to sign up for graphic design classes. I was filled with so much annoyance: I was trying to make a new hobby work and yet, I was not as satisfied as I knew I could be.

I discussed my feelings about my new classes with my mom and dad, and explained to them that I was scared that I wasn't feeling the same passion for graphic design as I had been with fashion design in prior years. I relayed that I was continuing to grow increasingly frustrated that it had now been two years and I still had no clue what else I could possibly want to do with my life. They reassured me, suggesting to me that I needed to stop trying so hard to find a rock-solid path. They reminded me that there was nothing wrong with not knowing what you want to do, and that millions of students go to college not knowing where they will end up. They explained to me that the whole point of life was to try new things and explore what the world around me has to offer. They helped me to realize that these graphic design classes were not there for me to lock myself into another "grand plan," but to explore other opportunities that might interest me as well.

Taking this information to heart, I decided to completely let go and not worry about any future plans or careers just yet. It was time for me to relax a bit and be okay with floating in limbo for a while. During this time, I tried courses in Basic Design, Digital Photography, Technical Theatre, Foreign Languages, and more! I had no idea I had so many other passions and hobbies bubbling underneath the surface that I enjoyed so much. I still had no idea what I wanted to do with my life, but I was having the time of my life not knowing, and just exploring what I had around me.

A few months later, I suddenly found a new passion that gave me the same feeling that fashion did as a little girl. To my surprise, it was probably one of the most "left field" ideas in which I could ever expect to invest myself. Toward the end of my junior year of high school, I was returning my textbooks to my school library and decided to look around a bit before I left. I don't go to the library very often, but as I looked up and down the shelves, I found a bright book that was about locations in England. My interest was piqued immediately, and I decided to give the book a try.

As I turned each page, I was filled with enchantment and allure while finding out more about places with which I was familiar, along with information about so many new places. I felt more and more intrigued by the world around me as I kept reading about cities like London, Doncaster, Manchester and more. I was mesmerized by the beautiful pictures of these areas. It was like I was staring into a dream. The book made me interested in finding out about other cities or towns around the world, so I looked for similar books. I spent a long time in the library that day, searching for information about places from France to Ireland to Spain, down to Australia, back up to Denmark, and more. As I sat there feeling a sense of wonder about these gorgeous areas, I took a minute to try to recognize the feeling that came over me. It brought me back to when I first fell in love with fashion design: a strong wave of love and passion that I had been craving and missing in my life for so long.

Feeling so excited about my new discoveries, I rushed home and began researching opportunities to travel to these stunning places. I eventually came across the idea of studying abroad. Through my research, I found a college that offered wonderful once-in-a-lifetime opportunities to study abroad. It was a nature-filled campus with an extraordinary variety of courses and programs. I scheduled a tour of the out-of-state campus and fell in love as I explored its offerings. I couldn't wait to apply!

The thought of going to college out of state and studying abroad became less scary and more exciting to me. This helped me understand that super-gluing myself to a plan and career for almost nine years made me subconsciously feel completely stuck in my own idea of what life should be. In turn, I blocked out any future possibilities for me to do anything else with my time. As I continued to think about what my life would have been like had I kept working toward my "grand plan" as an LA fashion designer, I became more and more aware of how unhappy I would have been. Suddenly, the idea of leaving the state I have lived in for my entire life felt like a breath of fresh air.

As I continued to picture this new life I was envisioning, I became more and more thrilled. At the same time, I realized that I was not actually creating a new career path like I had desperately tried to do over the past two years. I was only changing the place where I lived. And you know what? I was completely fine with that. The excitement of exploring something new was equally enticing (if not more so) than finding a new career to pursue. It was enough of a change for me to feel passionate about my life again, whether I had a career lined up or not. No longer was I feeling anxious or frustrated at the thought of not having a plan or feeling like I would be thrown out of high school for not having a clue what to do with my life. Instead, I was sitting comfortably in my junior year of high school feeling overjoyed at the possibility of exploring new countries and finding new opportunities somewhere else. I had found it. The key was to be passionate about my life as a whole, not merely about my career.

While this story follows the life of a 17-year-old thinking about college, my experience applies to anyone who is considering a career change, or someone who has begun to change their path but simply does not know where to go from here, or someone who feels the same way I felt and has no idea what they want to do to make a new start. My advice to you is to refrain from making any decision at all, and just explore all the opportunities and possibilities around you.

If you ever want to change your life but have no idea where to go from here, or if you feel how I felt and think you are running out of time to make a new plan for your life, I encourage you to be okay with not knowing what you want and to spend some time "floating" through life and just living. At some point, your path will find you.

Here are some questions you can ask yourself if you are struggling to find the passion in your life:

1. Are there any new hobbies I want to experience?

Although it is not currently what I want to do in my life, trying out classes like graphic design and photography allowed me to release small sparks of passion for things that I never let myself explore. Your new hobby doesn't need to be your career! Spend a couple of days, weeks, or even months just exploring little activities that you haven't had time to pursue. Whether you find a new path or not doesn't diminish the benefit of trying new things, and you will never waste your time building unique and enjoyable experiences for yourself.

2. Are there any new places I want to go?

Maybe you are like me and the change you need is a change in scenery! Remember, decisions like this don't need to be so extreme. If moving to a new country or state sounds too daunting for you now, it could be simply moving to a new town or neighborhood that speaks to you or in which you find yourself wanting to spend time. Even just eating at a restaurant that caught your eye on a side of town to which you have never been could introduce you to new stores, activities, and people that you find fascinating. A change in scenery might even bring your next path to you!

3. Do I just need some time to think or breathe?

If you have been working hard and emotionally pounding yourself into the ground while trying to plan out your life or career, it is easy to block your heart from making a meaningful decision. Let yourself think! Let yourself breathe! Whether that means hanging out with friends or being a couch potato for a few days, do what you need to do to give yourself room to consider what you truly want to explore. Part of living with passion in your life is doing what feels right in the moment, even if that means spending a few days doing nothing. Remember, "wasting time" is not wasted time. If it is beneficial to you, then you deserve it.

Not knowing what to do next is possibly the most powerful thing you can do for your life. By not knowing, you are allowing yourself to accept the variety of different opportunities available to you, and you are opening yourself to anything that comes your way. This allows you to refrain from selecting one path, but instead to accept all paths. By having this mindset and living each day as it comes, you unlock the key to ultimate success and happiness that truly has nothing to do with a career or any other life decision. Be passionate about living your life, and remain open to all it has to offer.

CHAPTER

Opportunity
By Rosanne Groover Norris

In 2020, Rosanne authored *beLEEve, A Journey of Loss, Healing, and Hope*, which was ranked number one in several categories, in both the U.S. as well as internationally. She is also contributing author to the anthology, *Ordinary Oneness, The Simplicity of Everyday Love, Grace, and Hope*, and *Gathering at the Doorway, An Anthology of Signs, Visits, and Messages from the Afterlife*, compiled by Camille Dan.

Rosanne and Lee were featured in the award-winning documentary, "Rinaldi," the story of Brazilian instrumental trans-communication researcher Sonia Rinaldi, who for over thirty years has brought through images and voices from deceased loved ones in spirit. "Rinaldi" is available on Prime Video, Vimeo, and Tubi.

BY ROSANNE GROOVER NORRIS

Rosanne is a reiki master, and a grief educator, certified by the world-renowned David Kessler.

She can be reached at rmnorris457@gmail.com

Chapter 5

Opportunity

By Rosanne Groover Norris

I've heard some parents say their child's death was a gift. Not me. Because if my son's death was a gift, I would want a refund. What I can say, however, is that my son's death provided an opportunity to change, grow, and find purpose in my life. I had to make a conscious choice to stay mired in my pain or find a way out. I wanted out. It wasn't an easy or linear process. I used many modalities to help navigate and absorb the grief into my life, and healing is now part of my life-long journey.

Grief is consuming, confusing, and erratic. It invades your entire being. I was not prepared for the unexpected, out-of-order death of my son. I was blindsided by the pain. I didn't know this kind of pain even existed. My son was dead, and the old me was dead, too. The joy, happiness, and beauty in my life left with my son. I wasn't sure I could go on living or even if I wanted to. I didn't care about anything or anyone, myself included. That first cold, gray winter after his death matched what I felt inside; cold, gray, numb, and lifeless. The pain felt lodged in my chest, at times making it hard to breathe. I sat and stared. I walked around in an aimless fog. I screamed and cried, curled in a ball on the floor. And I spent sleepless nights asking why this happened as I clutched his sweater, breathing in his smell.

It's easy to fall into the trap of masking our pain with drugs, alcohol or distracting ourselves with mindless activities because we live in a society that teaches us to avoid pain at all costs. I sometimes downed glass after glass of wine to suffocate my pain, but it only made it worse. I wasn't sure what to do next, but I knew I had to do something.

I had so many questions. Why did this happen? Where did my son go? Why are we here? And what do I do now? Then, one day I turned on the television for distraction. The Dr. Oz Show was on, and two doctors were speaking about their near-death experiences. It caught my attention. I listened as Dr. Eben Alexander and Dr. Mary Neal each told their story of how they died, and experienced the afterlife, then came back changed. These two hard-core scientists, who had no belief in life continuing after death before their experiences, were now convinced the afterlife was real. I was stunned. What prompted me to turn on the television, at that very moment, to a show I rarely watched? I wasn't sure, but I was intrigued. I started to read books related to death, the afterlife, near-death experiences, reincarnation, signs, and communications from our loved ones. Then I discovered podcasts to add to my reading.

I became a seeker.

I was open to everything in my path, but this didn't mean that I had to accept every new idea. When I first heard about soul plans, I thought to myself there was no way I would agree to my son leaving this world before me. I was indignant at the very suggestion. However, my viewpoint eventually softened. To think my son's death might be an agreement between us rather than a random, senseless incident now brings me a sense of comfort.

Along with the things I was learning, I began to employ various modalities to aid in my healing. Journaling, meditation, gratitude, spending time in nature, and mediums are some of the things that helped me to navigate my grief.

For most of my life, whenever I had a problem, I would work through it by writing, so journaling was a natural place for me to start. I filled page after page with rage and pain. I wrote about my hurt when people didn't mention him. Did they forget or not even care? I wrote about the people who avoided me in the grocery store by pretending to look at a list or turning around abruptly in the aisle. I felt like an outcast. I wrote about my anger when asked if I was enjoying retirement, which I took two months after my son passed. I wrote about my rage when someone said God needed my son more than me. I wondered what child he would be willing to give up. I also wrote about the things I questioned. Why did this happen to me? Can I survive this? Will I have to pretend I'm okay for the rest of my life? I also wrote about memories and the signs I was receiving, like the time we danced to "Rapper's Delight" at a family wedding. Or the time I glanced up from reading and saw my son's name written in the clouds.

I wrote letters to my son to process my feelings, but my grief counselor suggested I write a letter from my son to me. He said to put pen to paper and write it without thinking or stopping. And two months after his passing, I wrote these words. I believe they were channeled directly from my son.

Dear Mom,

I wish I could take it all back. I wish I could take away everyone's pain. I don't like to see you hurting so much. I'm sorry. I would change it if I could. I was careless but not purposely. I was lazy and distracted. I love you very much, and I am sorry I have hurt you. Please know I am safe and happy like never before. Everyone I know and love is here but you, but it's okay. Someday, you will see me again, but until then, I will be with you always, just not as you knew me. You will be okay. Mom, work through the grief and be gentle with yourself. Someday you will laugh again. I miss being with you and the family, but I was not meant to grow old. It was my time. I did struggle with life. So many things happened to me, and this was the biggest thing. But maybe it saved me from something worse down the road. I am safe. I am happy. I am loved. You will be okay.

All my love. Your son,

Lee

Journaling has helped me understand and accept how grief works. Grief is an up-and-down mixture of feelings, but no feeling is forever. Journaling has given me a nudge down my healing path.

I was familiar with meditation through my yoga practice, but now I turned to meditation as a healing tool. I learned to quiet my mind, be in the present moment, open my heart, and trust what I received. Meditation gave me peace. As I became a regular meditator, I started feeling tingling on the left side of my head, like bugs were crawling there. In time, I recognized it was my son, confirming he was with me. The tingling continues to happen, physically confirming what my heart knows is true. My son still lives. I also would hear, in my head, "I'm okay" or "I'm having the time of my life." At first, I thought I had made this up to console myself, but I learned to trust it was from him. During one meditation, I saw a Miniature Schnauzer in my mind's eye. I didn't recognize this dog, but later that day, I spotted him on a local breeder's site. And when I found out he was available on the very day my son had passed, I knew this dog was meant to be mine. This was no coincidence. I brought him home a few days later. Learning to trust what I received has given me hope and courage to continue on my healing journey.

I read how being grateful can help with healing. At first, it was hard to be grateful because my mind wanted to focus on what I lost. So, I started with simple things like the coffee I was drinking or that I had plenty of food to eat. However, I got a lesson in gratitude when I asked a mom how she had survived the death of her eight-month-old baby. She smiled and said, "I am thankful and smile every day because his life happened, and I was blessed to be his mom." I thought about the thirty years my son was in my life, and I felt real gratitude for the first time. Now I am grateful for so many things in my life. I am grateful I survived the worst thing in my life. I am grateful to know he lives a full life in a place called home. I am grateful for the wonderful people I have met who have helped me on this journey. And I am grateful my son lets me know he is with me, with tingles on my head and other signs he brings to my attention, like the number 34, which was his youth football number I see multiple times a day. Gratitude is a practice that helps me shift my focus from negative to positive thoughts. And I am grateful I have learned this.

I always enjoyed being outside and appreciated nature, but I discovered its healing power. I feel at peace being in nature. I open my eyes and heart, breathe, and take in the beauty. I listen to the wind move my chimes. I watch the birds going about their business. I send love to the trees that stand strong against the weather. I watch the lake, where I live, sparkle in the sunlight. I feel connected to the universe when I am in nature. I see an eagle or a hawk, and I am reminded of my soul's higher perspective. I feel part of nature, as a human and a spiritual being. I cannot change the past or know the future, but I can be grounded and in the present moment, in nature.

Medium readings were a crucial part of my healing work. Mediums gave me the proof I needed that my son was alive. I had at least two dozen readings in the first two years after my son transitioned and heard some incredible things that left no doubt in my mind my son was alive and well. The first reading I had was a few months after my son passed. He showed the medium Monopoly money. Growing up, he loved

Monopoly, and we played it frequently. Another one early on indicated there was something in the console of his car, which his sister now drove. She found a French fry there that was not hers. My son even shared things that hadn't happened yet, like a quilt that would be made from his shirts and the book I would write. He even suggested the title would be Belief or Beyond Belief, and it ended up being close. I am grateful for all of the mediums who have given me more than the validation my son is alive. They have given me the courage, hope, and comfort to carry on in this lifetime.

I don't believe we are meant to grieve in isolation. I felt I no longer fit in. I needed to be with people who understood my pain. I tried a grief group, but everyone seemed stuck in their grief even after many years. It was not helpful, and I left knowing I would not go back. It was early in my grief, but I knew I did not want to feel sad for the rest of my life. Through a search on Facebook, I found my tribe. Helping Parents Heal is an international organization for parents who have suffered the loss of a child. The group is open to discussion on spirituality and the afterlife, and they encourage communication with our children. The parents in the group do not call themselves bereaved but 'Shining Light Parents,' who shine through the healing love and connection with their children. This group felt right to me. I know I was led there by my son. Right after I joined this organization, I heard a dad speak about his grief from the loss of his son. He said, "I thought about my son and decided I wouldn't want my son to see his dad a sad and broken man." This was a pivotal moment for me, and his words went straight to my heart. I decided to live my life as best I could and make my son proud. I am grateful to have found the support I needed, and I now help other parents new to this journey.

I took the opportunity to learn, grow, and accept. Things I never knew or didn't give much thought to now make sense and even give me comfort, like soul plans, exit points, signs, connection, and communication with our loved ones. Through books, podcasts, journaling, meditation, and gratitude, I have shifted from hoping to believing to knowing the truth. We don't die. We change form, and we go home. I fully believe we come into human form with a life plan for growth, and we leave when there is an opportunity, and it's our soul's choice. I used to question why this happened, but that answer is no longer important to me. What is important is how I live my life. I am grateful to have found a path of healing to guide me along this journey. Grief is forever, but with determination, courage, and the right tools, you can live a life filled with hope, love, and joy while helping others along the way.

I have learned to be open to the universe and its divine plan. I have accepted things happen for reasons we might not understand. I trust I am guided by guides, angels, and loved ones on the other side of life. I believe the universe aligns situations and people in perfect timing rather than coincidences. I have learned to get out of my head, trust what I feel, and let my intuition guide me. I have grown more patient with myself and others in my life. I have filled my life with peace by not getting caught up in the news or gossip. I understand everything I say or do, affects everything else in a kind of ripple effect, and I will understand how I affect others when I go home. I try not to judge others because I cannot know their lesson for this lifetime. I am more forgiving of myself and others. I believe in our connection as human beings and the need to care for each other because love is all there is. I have learned to release the things that do not serve me, like worry, fear, and stress. I believe we each have unique gifts to share with the world. I spend more time in nature, and I now see it in a way I couldn't before. I am more thankful for the blessings and lessons in my life. I have learned it's okay to live, laugh, and love again. So, I say yes to life and everything it holds for me, the beauty, the joy, and the pain because I believe we are here to experience and learn from it before we go back home.

We all are wounded, bearing scars, and carrying our crosses, but knowing we are all connected at a soul level helps us feel less alone, and helping others helps us to heal. I will always carry grief in my heart because I am human, but my growth has led me to a point where I can exist in peace for the rest of my life, knowing I will see my son again. I will live my life helping others. I will spread love, compassion, and kindness. I will speak my truth. I will shine my light. I will be happy. I will be joyful. And I will never stop seeking.

Buddist monk, and teacher, Thích Nhất Hạnh says, "Do not fight against pain. Embrace it as though you are embracing a little baby." I have met my pain head-on, walked through it, and come out the other side baptized new. This is the mom I want my son to see. Maybe that's the gift.

May you find your way out of darkness to discover peace, joy, and purpose. Namaste.

CHAPTER Six

Forever with You: How to Ignite Your Truth, Discover Your Joy, and Belong
By Donna Kiel

Donna Kiel is a thought leader, wisdom teacher, change maker and a guide for those seeking their best life. Donna has a unique ability to inspire you to discover and live your highest potential. Donna's expertise and training, along with her engaging and welcoming persona, provide others with the compassion and connection needed to discover their own genius and passion. Donna is a coach, mentor, best-selling author, professor, and architect of change who works for equity and empathy in every context. Donna holds a doctorate in educational leadership and is a certified counselor, life coach, and is certified in Whole Brain Living.

Donna created the empathy framework with practical tools to lead individuals and organizations to experience new levels of connection, creativity, and success. Donna is often sought for innovative change efforts by organizations and individuals seeking solutions to systemic and life challenges. Donna inspires, enlivens, and creates useful and practical solutions. Donna is the epitome of inspiration and integrity for those seeking meaning, insight, and concrete answers to the next steps in life. Donna is currently a professor, speaker, coach, and mentor offering workshops, individual coaching, anxiety relief, career planning, and life mapping sessions.

Donna can be reached at drdonnakiel@gmail.com or through her website at https://donnakiel.com

Chapter 6

Forever with You

By Donna Kiel

Most mornings, I wake up and calculate how many hours until I can finally do what I want to do. How many tasks, meetings, errands, and conversations do I have to get through until I get to that blissful part of the day that is all mine? The thing is that the blissful part of the day most often happens just before sleep when I'm so exhausted, I cannot do one more thing or summon the energy to even name what it is I want to do. I typically fall into a restless sleep, saying tomorrow will be different. Tomorrow I will make time for me, time to write, time to relax, or time to find that elusive meaning of life. The statement, "Tomorrow I will have time for me, or tomorrow will be better," is a warning sign. It is the red flag that I've fallen into the abyss of avoiding my life rather than living my life.

Have you noticed that you, too, are always waiting for the moment that is yours? Have you put your wants and needs so far down on the list that they are now not recognizable? Are you waiting to get that "to-do" list done before you experience joy? Are you, like me, endlessly searching self-help books for the pathway out of the familiar "after this, then I will."? Are you searching for that truth of where you should be in life and what path is really for you?

If you are, I want to share with you two important strategies to move out of waiting for life to happen and move into igniting the truth of your inner joy that creates authentic belonging. What I will share with you is the culmination of my own life experiences, my research, and an examination of how we can fully live our best lives to be lives of meaning, impact, love, and joy.

First, the fact is that you can't hide from the truth. That reality can be scary. However, while you can't hide from the truth, the truth can hide from you. The truth can play the best game of hide and seek with a hint there is something more and then the disappearance behind the busyness of life. Truth can be very annoying and downright masterful in allowing our fears to take over and silence the true desires we have. You know your truth is in there. You can hear it in the whispers of your heart, and yet you can't seem to always find it. Your truth, like my truth, can bury itself deeply inside of you, creating an illusion of life. That truth of who you are and what your life is destined to become turns into a torturous unsettled feeling that permeates your being.

For much of my life, I lived in the "after this" mindset. After this, I'll find time to write something just for me. After this event, I can relax and read what I want at my own pace. After I get this part of the house fixed, then I'll feel better and enjoy the space. After I have this much money, I won't worry anymore. After, after, after. The thinking of "after this" is an artful denial of the opportunities life offers us to live authentically.

"After this" consumed me and became so habitual and ingrained that I never realized I wasn't experiencing true joy. "After this" had created inconsolable levels of anxiousness, worry, and rage. I resented every single item on a to-do list I created. I got angry when people I scheduled to meet with me actually met with me. I was filled with fear that I would not be able to get everything done and would lose the job I was beginning to despise. I was scared, angry, detached, and lost in waiting and attempting to keep up with a fast-paced, overwhelming, and time-consuming daily existence.

In one seemingly routine moment with my precious four-year-old granddaughter Charlie, all of that changed. As I looked at my phone after seeing a text fly in and then looked to see how much more time I was scheduled to be with her, Charlie said, "Hey, look here!"

I felt this wash of shame, regret, and intense fear. I realized "after this" had stolen my soul, buried my truth, and created a misery I could no longer endure. I was with her and thinking well, after this, I can get to that text. It was a heartbreaking realization. You see, I deeply adore my granddaughter, Charlie. Each time I am with her, I feel this deep feeling of belonging and joy. It is a feeling I have longed for my entire life. It is a belonging that is not based on who I am or what degree I hold, or what I can do for her. It is the purest, most precious, and most vulnerable type of belonging and love. The deep love I have for Charlie can take my breath away. I didn't realize until that moment that this deep feeling of joy was also scaring the hell out of me. Why would I be looking at my watch and thinking "after this" when I was with her? I loved being with her. Yet, I was looking at time with her as yet another "after this" to get through to do the next thing on my list and looking at that next thing as the next thing. My life was not my life—it was a list.

In a flash, something whispered to me—this moment is not forever. The embarrassment and shame that this precious four-year-old had to call me out on not being present were demoralizing. Fear gripped my soul as the truth of my mortality washed over me with overwhelming panic that suffocated me. NO! I don't want to lose one moment of belonging and love with Charlie. I want time to stand still. Each time I look into her eyes or feel her arms wrap around my leg, I long for that moment to remain forever. But time doesn't stand still, nor does the reality that life will end.

My fear of loss and rejection has dominated each decision I've made in life and now was present with me as I was with Charlie. My fear is very powerful. My fear motivates me to get things done, to say yes when I want to say no and to try to answer work texts when I want to be with Charlie. My fear is a strong director guiding my every move with orders that are insistent that I must do what it says.

In defense of my very determined fear, that fear is always attempting to protect me from some impending doom. My fear, I call her Frances after my mother because my fear's goal is to make sure I am doing what the world says I should, just as my mother did. Frances, both my mother and my fear, want to protect me from experiencing the rejection, bullying, embarrassment, and pain I felt as a child and adolescent. Frances is powerful and amazingly adept at high levels of organization and functioning. That fear created and still creates my unending to-do lists, has great ideas for new work projects to support other people's purpose and truth, and is the best at scheduling my time so fully that each day is never time or space for me to be quiet enough to listen to the whispers of what I wanted to do or to feel the pain that love is also often loss.

Luckily for you and me, our truth cannot be hidden forever. The challenge for all of us is allowing our truth to change us.

For me, I've come to realize that my truth and my life are not in agreement. I believed I had created a path for myself that honored my potential and reflected purposeful clarity. I had done all the things that someone "should" do. I went to college, got married, got a job as a counselor to make a difference, had kids, and put on all the roles I was supposed to. Yet I always felt this ache expressed as sorrow, anxiety, and rage. I couldn't undo the person I had become who was this driven professional that others would describe as a "workhorse" and selfless. I couldn't ever find the courage to say no to any request—personal or professional. And when I felt afraid, which is often, I started searching for the next credential I could add to validate my existence. Yet even a doctorate and university appointments didn't seem enough.

Now, as I look back, in the sixth decade of my life, I finally realize I said yes and became that workhorse and selfless person to get the love, approval, and belonging that I desperately wanted.

Igniting your joy, purpose, and belonging requires pausing long enough to discover what it is that you are searching for beneath the role, the job, the work, and the people. For me, the loss I felt of my mother's attention and love after the birth of my Down syndrome brother created an urgency to ensure that I would not be rejected, abandoned, or shamed as I was back then. I became that overachiever to calm the fears that were instilled so very young.

I avoided loss by focusing on what I needed to do to fix each area of my life. I distracted from the distress of realizing with love comes loss, by working so hard to convince others to admire me and becoming, in my mind, someone they needed and could not live without.

My vulnerable little soul convinced herself it was easier to stay busy than to feel the deep and frightening pain that comes with limitless and eternal loving. It was easier to book my time from waking until exhaustion than to be present with myself enough to feel all the feelings.

We humans often need a breakdown to have a breakthrough. I also think that God, the universe, or divine intervention—whatever you may call it—sends each of us messages to push that truth up to the surface. I had to have several breakdowns before I had that breakthrough. I seemed too often to ignore those nudges.

A recent health scare shook me just long enough to temporarily have me go back to meditation, writing, and painting—things I love to do. But that was fleeting as my wonderful fear took charge again and dove me back into working and doing. Budget cuts at the university and the threat of losing my position as professor shook me long enough to re-examine what I wanted to contribute to life, but that, too, was temporary as my position was secured. Each little tap on the shoulder provided by God's whisper of "wake up" was a short-lived interruption to my fear avoidance dance. That was until that moment with Charlie when I realized joy and love can hurt as deeply as loss and rejection. If I were to feel deeply the love and joy of people I care about, I would also need to feel the agonizing fear that I can lose it all at any moment and that life is uncertain.

I wanted from life what I was giving Charlie. I wanted someone, mostly my mother, to give me that undistractable attention, the unshakable acceptance, and the forever love that creates a permanent sense of belonging.

Step One – Fear

Finding truth requires the first step of naming our fear. When was the first time in your life that you felt afraid—really afraid? What was happening, and how did the fear change you? Fear is almost always born of feelings of losing what you feel you desperately need.

To discover the impact of that fear, ask yourself what feeling it is that you want more than anything else in your life. What feeling do you never want to lose? What feeling is so completely blissful that you are broken open to overwhelming fear at the thought of losing it? I've learned it is not what we "want" in life that determines our true purpose and path; it is what "feeling" we desire to experience—that is most important in experiencing our purposeful life, authentic joy, and the reality that we are where we belong.

As I look back on the choices in my life, I can see that so many were choices designed to make someone else accept me and choose me to be part of their lives so I could feel worthy. I never could seem to fully access and choose the path that was authentically mine. Instead, I would very discretely, almost with intentional pretense, follow a path that fit a culture mold and also let me, just a little bit, have what I wanted.

For example, when I became a school principal, I knew I wanted to help kids. What I wanted was for those I admired to admire me and think I mattered. My mom died shortly before I became a principal. My fear blocked the overwhelming grief of losing her by getting a job that would keep me busy from dawn to dusk. I wanted my mom to be proud, to say I mattered, and to love me and be with me forever. The truth was I didn't want to work in the principal world of structure and policy implementation. Being a principal wasn't enough and didn't fill that need, so I got a doctoral degree and became a professor. I could again fill up my schedule, create a masterfully busy life and get angry I never had time for myself. The result was overwhelming anxiety driving me into therapy.

In countless sessions with my therapist, I expressed how anxious and fearful I felt. My therapist would ask me what was the worst that could happen if my fears came true. I would get annoyed and say the same things about getting fired or being abandoned. She would reply, "Yes, and then what?" And session after session, my therapist would surface my mother. I was annoyed. I kept saying, she's dead, and I'm over that. Very wisely and skillfully, she knew my search for purpose and meaning was evidence I was not over her, but rather I was holding incredible anger at her.

She gave me that opportunity for yet another breakdown to gain a breakthrough. One question from my therapist broke me down and broke through. She asked, "What if the fear and anxiety you are experiencing is not yours—what if this is your mother's story?" It was my mother's legacy. She was afraid I would be rejected, hurt, or not belong. I had crafted my life to honor my mother's fears, and my truth was angrily trying to be spoken.

For as long as I can remember, I've been angry and distant from my mom. I adored her grace, charm, and passion for life, and I resented the way she pushed me, seemed to love everyone else more than me, and the way she was afraid of everything. I blamed her for my own need to hide away from life. I blamed her for dying suddenly and leaving me with my dad even though I was in my forties. I blamed her for not giving me a chance to tell her the truth about who I was.

My rage and deep love for her had blocked my truth. I needed to make my way to forgiving her to set free and honor my truth.

One day, as I was playing with Charlie and allowing myself to be present at the moment, out of nowhere, I whispered, "Mom, you would love her so much—I wish you were here." It was the first time in the 20 years since her sudden death that I wished her back with the authentic, forever love that defined the truth of my being. I deeply love my mother, and her spirit, her essence, and even her anxiety is an essential part of my truth.

Step Two – Forgiveness

The second step to igniting your joy and meaningful life is forgiveness. Who do you need to forgive? What anger, sorrow, grief, or fear are keeping you from your truth? I needed to forgive my mother. At that moment with Charlie, I not only forgave her, but I also permitted myself to love her. But I also needed and still need to forgive myself. I'm cruel to myself in ways I would never be to anyone else. If you are a demanding, relentless, and critical boss to you—stop now. Forgive what you may have perceived as not good enough in you. Igniting your joy and path to meaning requires forgiving the misplaced judgment you have of yourself. Forgive you and give yourself the unconditional, open-hearted, welcoming, and forever love you deserve.

Igniting your truth and discovering your joy and belonging wherever you are requires fear and forgiveness. Put away the distractions of work, social media, to-do lists, and busyness. Embrace the present moment. Allow fear to wash over you and allow yourself to feel as if you are drowning—just stay there and feel. Those deep, uncomfortable feelings are the beautiful part of life that is needed to feel that incredible joy that is only yours. Realize, as I have, that those you love are yours to love, and they are forever with you. Embracing your fear and finding forgiveness can transform your life and ignite each day with meaning and love that says love and purpose are forever, and you belong exactly where you are.

CHAPTER Seven

Standing At The Cliff's Edge
By Becki Koon

Becki Koon is an International Bestselling Author and Speaker, Heart-based Energy Intuitive, Holy Fire III® Karuna Reiki Master, HeartMath® Coach, Life Coach, ThetaHealer, Crystal Practitioner, and ULC Minister. Through her business, Step Stone, Becki empowers people to seek their inner wisdom while holding space for them to discover, and grow into the next highest version of themselves, and she does this through compassionate love. Becki views her service in the world as a sacred offering.

Becki's work evolved in a way she never expected. When her husband of 12 years passed, she knew her life was forever changed. She did not expect she would wake up to the capability of communication with him through mediumship. Now, in her sessions, Becki receives guidance from him, Jesus, her angelic guides, her family of light, other people's guides, loved ones who've passed, and ascended masters. Channeling is a gift she says helped her deal with loss, grief, and her own health challenges.

Being in service to others has given Becki an outlet for the compassionate wisdom she gained. Conscious death, afterlife channeling, and self-love through a cancer diagnosis have changed her life, work, and very essence. She vows to continue using the gifts she has been encouraged to remember and offers to the world her passion for living a sacred and divinely guided life. She thanks God for every breath she takes.

Contact:

stepstone2you@gmail.com

www.beckikoon.com

www.facebook.com/becki.koon.consulting

amazon.com/author/beckikoon

Chapter 7

Standing At The Cliff's Edge

By Becki Koon

Who knew that discovering a passage into the deep waters of passion could be found by swimming in the dark corridors of a life-threatening diagnosis like cancer? We have all heard stories of people finding new purpose when faced with life-and-death situations. It is entirely understandable how a traumatic event can change someone thrown into the midst of life-altering conditions. But to know it in your own body, hearing the words bounce around your eardrum, is a surreal experience.

My cell phone rang as I had just entered the back seat of my kids' car. It was a call from my doctor. "Becki, the lab results are in. I hate to tell you this, but it is confirmed; you have stage 3 invasive ductile carcinoma in your left breast. We need to immediately get you set up with oncology to explore your options. I will make the necessary calls. I'm so sorry."

I was with my daughter, son-in-law, and my two granddaughters, heading to my mom's place for Memorial Day Weekend. It had been 20 months since my husband, Jack, left this life with a cancer diagnosis. The word rang raw in my ears, and the blood seemed to rush out of my body as I took in the news. Tears started to well in my daughter's eyes while I took a breath and allowed the wave of shock to wash over me. I looked at my granddaughters, who were too young to understand, and I smiled and said, "Well then, I know what I am dealing with now. It is going to be okay." Fascinating how shock can react in the human body's emotional, physical, mental, and spiritual aspects.

Two years have passed since receiving the news on that day, but the memory of the moment is entrenched into the recesses of my psyche, and I can relive the body's response in a heartbeat. Moments like that can get burned into the very essence of who we are as a soul in this human form. Honoring complex human responses to our life experiences is a heartfelt passion I feel for the human condition we all share. My premise is based on a belief in a divine soul within physical form, the marriage of an everlasting soul finding human life through a human body designed to witness the power of that sacred marriage.

We are beautifully complex and simple all at the same time. The myriad of emotions we feel through this body is miraculous. Yet, a traumatic event can throw us into an internal storm taking on the unique characteristics of an individual lifetime experience. All recorded personal history can get rolled up into one moment of immense energetic power, a singular reality of epic proportions affecting our emotional, physical, mental, and spiritual bodies.

That power can impact the emotional body through feelings of shock, fear, sadness, grief, numbness, dissociation, and so on and so forth. Again, the emotions are as unique to each soul as the grains of sand on a beach. The commonality is that we are human and have the beautiful capacity to feel emotions; even when they hurt, and we want them to go away, we don't want to feel them. The courageous soul feels whatever is happening at the moment without self-judgment. Not easy, an almost impossible task in the nucleus of a traumatic storm.

That power can impact our physical body. Instant heat can raise our internal temperature causing beads of sweat to form on the skin. Tingles can run up and down the spine while the breath can become constricted, making it hard to breathe, feeling like a weight is sitting on the chest. The stomach can respond with nausea and butterflies feel like they have just taken flight. Muscles can spasm and tears erupt as if relieving an internal pressure valve about to explode. Or on the flip side, numbness can wash over and the body feels stagnant, non-responsive, and deadened.

That power can send the mental body into overdrive, racing through thoughts and mind chatter to find stable ground when everything stable has been yanked out from under you. Your thinking can become clouded, and you only want to find safety, a place to navigate your mind to help deal with the onslaught of danger signals released by past experiences. Your survival mind wants nothing but to keep you alive and will hijack rational thinking in milliseconds. The capacity for clear thinking is washed away in the flood of mental noise.

That internal storm's power can send the spiritual body into flight, questioning the existence of a God or divine connection. How could this be happening to me? Why am I experiencing this reality when all I do comes from goodness, love, and light? Am I a divine soul in form? Who am I? The denial of your inner awareness or soul essence can begin to express through body tightness, aches, and pain finding a place to lodge the suppression of your divine light in the cells of your physical form. Natural energy flow becomes blocked and the body's wisdom does everything to help you weather the rising reservoir of uncertainty behind the dam.

As a deeply spiritual, heart-based intuitive and empathic person, my work is immersed in the realm of energy management, human potential, and the spiritual dimensions we have access to. I have always felt the presence of Jesus near me after having an awakening in my early teen years. My career choice led me down the path of service to others through Reiki, HeartMath®, Crystal Healing, Ministerial work, Energy Dowsing, and Life Coaching. I have many excellent coping tools at my disposal.

And yet, in my very human moment of internal storm, I was taken away by the tumultuous winds that blasted the news of cancer into my personal story. I recognized I was beautifully human, flawed and perfect, but only after I had experienced the impact of the word cancer in all of my bodies, as mentioned earlier. Hence and to this day, the entrenched memory of the moment when I heard the news is written in my cells. How I defined my cancer story and my human moment was mine and mine alone.

I had some decisions to make; I was at a crossroads. Could I find it within me to navigate this storm?

I allowed my emotions to find flow and did not ignore nor did I suppress those feelings. I needed to enable the shock to move through me. I knew I was strong, but a rumbling deep within my soul questioned my desire to stay on the planet. My grief over losing my husband was something I learned to move through. I had no choice. But I often wondered how I could live life without him. My internal compass was pointing to the heavens and in my questioning moments, I wasn't sure if my journey would be the same as my husband's or that of survival. I needed help beyond my humanness. I needed my divine essence to guide me. So, I prayed.

I asked Jesus to hold my hand through the dark corridors to the dimly lit passage of internal strength. In my weakest moment, I fell to my knees and spoke to my husband, Jack, who I had seen in his glorious afterlife essence standing beside Jesus.

I knew I had to find my reason to remain because I was dancing between the worlds, not really grounded in the physical realm, wanting to stay in the in-between, feeling the bliss beyond the veil calling me, haunting me. I knew I had a life-or-death decision to make. My physical body was gifting me the opportunity to make a choice. I had to let go of my yearning for my husband in the physical and non-physical, at an even deeper, more profound level. I knew the rumbling storm represented my internal questioning. Immediately, I felt my children, my family, my friends, and my potential with another man. I could hear my husband pleading with me to stay, to love my life beyond him. At that moment, I found myself and I knew the decision. With my heart completely open, exposed, and raw, I sat on my knees in front of his picture and spoke to him through broken sobs while I let the tears stream down my face.

"I have to let you go, my love. Not a letting go of our divine, sacred love connection but a moving on in my current reality. I have to let go of my physical yearning for you in a way that challenges the very core of me, and yet I desire to live! I want my life here, Jack, and while I know you will never leave me, I want my life. I choose my life here on the planet. I choose to step into another love with a man when it presents itself. I am not done. Please help me to LIVE. God, please, help me to LIVE. WITH EVERY FIBER OF MY BEING, I CHOOSE LIFE! Jesus, please show me the way."

I let the moment take me into full body release. I knew this declaration was my commitment to life. I felt relief wash over me as if a large obstacle was lifted out of the way of forward movement. This declaration meant full steam ahead into the uncharted waters of the next few months.

Did I use all the tools I taught others? Yes, every last one of them and many more I would explore while I walked, and sometimes crawled, the path to wellness. I dove into my life experience in a way I never dreamed possible and documented the learning through my bestselling book, *Breathe The Deep Waters Of Love, A Dive Into Loss, Grief, Afterlife Connection, Self-Love and Living Life Forward.*

Standing at the cliff's edge of life can change a person. It is easy to see how being forced into action can help someone make a decision. It is like some unseen force pushing you into either annihilation or passion for survival. Most will choose survival and make every change necessary to stay the course. But what about the person who is not faced with a life-and-death scenario? How does the average person find the internal compass and fortitude to discover and unleash a passion for life?

This question has been ever present in my service to others. I stepped into a decision for life. I was blessed with an unwavering connection to the divine, like a mainline of energy from God to me. My life became a walking prayer and my zest for living was a gift I vowed to share with the world. The more I surrendered to divine guidance, the stronger the light within me grew and the inner flame of gratitude radiated out for all to witness. I humbly embodied more compassion, love, and light and my purpose was inflamed with the awareness of the beautiful inheritance God has given to all who breathe each breath of life.

With my clients, I began exploring what it meant to embrace their human bodies' emotional, physical, mental, and spiritual essences, the unique and beautiful aspects of each combining to create the whole being. My ignited flame was being used to spark the inner flame of others. How did we do it?

One of the most important keys I have found in my heart-based energy management business is the recognition of the divine within. We are all connected energetically, part of the fabric of this beautiful human classroom. As such, we are human physical forms embodied with a divine soul essence connected to God, source energy. My clients and I have found to embrace passion fully; integration of awareness to the divine within is the launch point. For me, there is no separation of physical and divine. It is all part of the whole of who we are. If you are alive, you have divinity within you. The expression of the divinity within is gauged by how strong the signal is dialed in. And, believe it or not, we are the ones who are in control of the dial.

Often you can feel it in your body when divine awareness enters. Many people will get tears in their eyes, chills might run up and down the spine, or the heart will feel energy. Sometimes it can be unnerving to feel the body respond to an unseen energy force moving through. I am there to remind clients it is okay to feel and experience what their body is showing them. It is the union of the divine within the body where magic begins to happen.

Many were not trained in subtle body awareness and feeling what it feels like to sense the waves of energy moving through. One of the ways I help my clients feel that subtle movement is through breath, breathing into the heart, placing a hand on the chest, imagining the heart breathing in and out, and picturing the breath moving into and down through the body. To feel the subtle shifts of energy, our higher essence needs to be embodied. A way to do that is through conscious body breath.

Once a person can acknowledge the divine within and feel the subtle energy shifts in the body, the unfolding discovery of who they are and what ignites their light has begun. Sometimes we must travel through many storms en route. The beautiful thing is that we are not traveling alone, no matter how isolated we feel. In one breath, we can access our soul, which is not separate from anyone or anything. When in proximity to another person holding the light of compassion, the energy of that compassion infiltrates and permeates the energy field around both, amplifying the energetic potential for all, and the storms lose power and focus. The safe route to inner purpose is illuminated and the entire unfolding is held by a loving God who guides the way.

As I mentioned, I have had a very close relationship with Jesus, but truthfully, I am fully aware God gave me a second chance at living. There is a knowing in every fiber of my being; my purpose was to experience all I have in this life to be the vessel through which the light of God can shine. It's not easy to describe the magnitude of that awareness in words, but it is clear to me; when I step into the higher energies of divine love and light, my body cells respond, healing takes place, and life force vitality is imbued and then released into the world. It is up to me to see the gift of this life and then share it in the many ways I can while serving the world.

A Chakra energy practitioner once told me my throat chakra was one of the strongest of all my energy centers and was directly linked to my heart. I must understand what that means for me and how I express it. We all have unique gifts, gifts our divine soul essence is ready to show the world. Can we step out of the boat onto the water and walk? What holds us back? Can we acknowledge who we are as divine creative beings having a human experience?

It is not up to me to tell anyone how to navigate their life. I can only offer support, suggestions, compassion, and example to others. I desire that you do not have to walk in my shoes to find a passion for life, to ignite your soul into a purpose-driven life. I hope knocking on death's door is a distant reality for you and that you find the magic of breathing life through other means, perhaps a chance encounter with another person or a moment of spiritual enlightenment.

Every day we can perceive life from the eyes of divinity, calling upon the interconnectedness of all things, aware of how our soul reaches out and touches another. May the energy touch we make with someone be filled with the compassion of Christ as we fully harmonize our human experience with that of eternal soul essence. It is a known fact when two or more gather in focused prayer and intention, the world is changed.

Nine months after my diagnosis, I was completely cancer free. My journey was not a passage into the next form of life but to stay firmly rooted on the planet, integrating the wisdom gained along the way. I took the route that made sense for me and, like an excited student, took the lessons I needed to ignite my passion even more fully. Out of that passion, the desire to share with others continues to blossom and life force energy expands and grows.

How long I have on this beautiful planet, I know not. None of us really know how long we have in these bodies. So, how about while we are here, we find within us the path to an enlightened living, expanding our awareness into the divine aspects we share, loving unabashedly, with complete abandon? I chose to live with the storms of life, to dance in the rain, hear the melody of rolling thunder, be in awe of the power of lightning, see the beauty of swirling winds, breathe the air that is gifted in every moment, and ignite the flame of life for all to be warmed by.

Take my hand. Let me hold space for you while we discover the spark within. Will you blow on that divine spark and fan the flame of passion within you? The time is now. Spirit is calling us into a purposeful and sacred life.

CHAPTER Eight

The Awakening of Purpose
By Pedram Owtad

With a deep dedication to family, personal growth, and contributing to society, I have happily embraced a married life for over 18 years, blessed with two precious sons aged 11 and 4.

As a computer engineer with an innate fascination for technology and innovation, I established CompuTech-Net over 28 years ago, committed to providing peace of mind through reliable technology solutions, and paradoxically, my passion has always been intertwined with the study of human behavior and spirituality.

BY PEDRAM OWTAD

Believing in the inherent goodness within each person and the positive aspect in every situation, I shared my life experiences on this subject at the esteemed event DebX, delivering a talk titled "Life is happening For us, and not To us," which has been documented in details as a chapter of the book, *When I Rise, I Thrive.*

Driven by an unwavering passion for meditation and a relentless quest for self-discovery, I began sharing my experiences by leading visualization meditations at monthly gatherings called "Together Just Be." The profound impact of these sessions led me to a greater calling—to bring the transformative power of meditation to a wider audience. Thus, the inception of "Unity Meditation" took place.

Guided by timeless questions such as "Who am I?" and "What is my purpose in life?" I embarked on a remarkable journey of self-realization and empowerment. The past decade has brought forth fascinating revelations, one of which has been eloquently shared in the book, *Wisdom Keepers.*

Now, in this book, *Ignite Your Fire Within*, I aim to illuminate a core question that has ignited my passion and bestowed upon me a profound understanding of my life's purpose.

It is with great honor that I share these insights, recognizing that asking the right question can illuminate our path and illuminate the inner callings we all seek. By finding the answers, we come to realize the extraordinary power, purpose, and preciousness that resides within every one of us as human beings.

Through my work, I aspire to inspire individuals to embark on their transformative journeys, unlocking their inner potential and embracing their unique purpose in life.

Stay diving,

Namaste

Pedram Owtad
info@unitymeditation.com
owtad@computechnet.com

Chapter 8

The Awakening of Purpose

By Pedram Owtad

WHY? – The ultimate question for the awakening of purpose.

In the depths of our existence lies a burning desire, a yearning for something greater than ourselves. It is a quest that permeates our thoughts, whispers in our dreams, and ignites a fire within our souls. The search for purpose is a universal endeavor, one that has the power to transform our lives and the lives of those around us. In this chapter, I invite you to join me on a personal journey of self-discovery as I share the transformative experiences that ignited my inner fire and led me to embrace passion and purpose.

The Call of the Soul

From an early age, the meaning of my existence beckoned me with persistent inquiries. It fueled a profound journey of self-discovery, guided by the question: *"What is my purpose and potential in this life?"* This inquiry became my compass, urging me to delve deeper into the recesses of my being.

In my exploration, I discovered that my gift lay in the realm of imagination, particularly when intertwined with the ethereal world of sound and music. Through the vibrations of melodies, a vivid tapestry of images unfolded before me, forging a deep connection to the world around me.

Though I pursued music passionately, I accepted that virtuosity eluded me. Yet, I found solace in music's power to ignite my imagination, becoming a conduit for my creative faculties. This revelation led me to the realm of meditation.

At just 11 years old, I embarked on an inner journey, guided by harmonious vibrations. These sacred sojourns offered me extraordinary experiences, such as ethereal out-of-body experiences and the awakening of dormant healing abilities, and more. Each encounter fueled my passion and deepened the quandary: how did this gift align with my unknown purpose?

Driven by an insatiable desire for answers, I pursued knowledge and introspection. I sought to unravel the tapestry that intertwined music, spirituality, and purpose. Each revelation stoked the fire within, propelling me to explore the depths of my soul.

Yet, uncertainty persisted amidst profound experiences and fervent passion. The connection between my abilities and purpose remained elusive. This paradox beckoned me further into self-discovery, embracing the unknown with an unwavering spirit.

Embracing My Dual Passions

In addition to my profound connection to music and spirituality, I found myself irresistibly drawn to the world of technology and innovation. The intricate workings of computers and the boundless possibilities they held fascinated me to no end. Driven by an insatiable curiosity, I decided to pursue a career in Computer Engineering, diving headfirst into the challenges and problem-solving nature of the field. While some may perceive technology and spirituality as divergent paths, I saw them as complementary facets of my multidimensional nature.

As I delved deeper into my journey, I discovered that computer graphics and 3D modeling provided an avenue for me to bring my imaginative visions to life tangibly and visually. It became a medium through which I could express and share the intricate tapestry of my inner world with others. The fusion of technology, creativity, and spirituality became a harmonious symphony that resonated deep within me, fueling my passion and guiding my endeavors.

Building a Life of Success and Stuff

Armed with graduate degrees in Computer Engineering, I established my own computer company, chasing the conventional markers of success: car, house, and material possessions that society deems valuable. Yet, amidst the trappings of success, the question that had plagued me since childhood persisted: *"What am I doing here?"*

Material achievements and possessions proved insufficient in answering the burning question that haunted me. A deeper yearning for meaning emerged from within, compelling me to unveil a dormant purpose.

External validation and material abundance served as fleeting distractions, unable to fulfill the profound answers my soul sought. The pursuit of purpose became a passionate quest, delving into the essence of my existence.

Amid societal expectations and the allure of possessions, I longed to strip away the layers of constructed identity. Unveiling my true self became a sacred pilgrimage, illuminating the path to my ultimate purpose.

Interweaving music, technology, spirituality, and self-exploration, I glimpsed the interconnectedness of these facets. Each passion held a piece of the purpose puzzle, guiding me to align my talents with a higher calling.

These reflections stoked the ember of my inner fire, igniting the recognition of a profound purpose awaiting me. With courage, I embarked on a transformative journey of self-discovery, shedding superficial expectations to uncover the truth within.

The path ahead was unknown, yet I embraced it wholeheartedly, knowing that the answers resided in the depths of my soul.

The Storm That Strengthened

Life, with its intricate tapestry of experiences, often puts us to the test, revealing our strengths and weaknesses in the most unexpected ways. It has a way of unfolding with a touch of irony, presenting challenges and tribulations that push us to the brink. And so it was that a tempestuous storm swept through my life, leaving no aspect untouched. It devoured my energy, depleted my savings, shattered my dreams, and disrupted the carefully laid plans that I had envisioned for myself. It felt as though everything I had diligently built was crumbling before my very eyes.

During this tumultuous period, where despair seemed to overshadow any glimmer of hope, I found solace in the understanding that the crucible of hardship has a unique way of shaping our character and revealing our true purpose. Adversity has a way of forging resilience, and resilience has a way of revealing purpose.

Amidst the chaos and despair, a question unfolded before me that was more profound than knowing my purpose, and it became the guiding light that illuminated my path: *"Who am I as a spiritual being?"* guiding me to rebuild and align actions with a higher calling.

In the darkness, my inner fire glowed brighter, stripping distractions and illusions to reveal my true self. With renewed purpose, I embraced the next chapter, ready to unlock hidden secrets.

Embracing the Inner Journey

The tempestuous storm became an irresistible call to embark on a profound odyssey of self-reflection and introspection. It urged me to reconnect with the passions that had flickered within me since childhood, igniting a fire that burned brighter than ever before. With unwavering determination, I plunged into the realms of spirituality and meditation, seeking solace and wisdom.

In this sacred exploration, I discovered that my purpose transcended the realm of external achievements and societal expectations. It resided in the depths of embracing my authentic self and embracing the profound gifts that I possessed. This transformative shift in mindset swung open the doors to a universe of boundless possibilities, igniting a relentless spark of curiosity deep within my soul. I realized that purpose was not a static destination to be reached, but an ongoing expedition of growth and self-realization. It beckoned me to explore the intricate dance of giving and receiving, to surrender to the eternal ebb and flow of energy that permeates the cosmos.

The Birth of *The Secret Cycle of Givers & Receivers*

Driven by this newfound understanding, I embarked on a path of self-reflection and introspection. As I delved into the depths of my own experiences, I uncovered a profound truth: the secret to unlocking our purpose lies in recognizing the interconnectedness of all beings. We are not isolated entities but threads in the intricate tapestry of existence, each contributing to the larger whole.

Inspired by this revelation, I began penning the pages of *The Secret Cycle of Givers & Receivers*, a book exploring the interconnected roles of givers and receivers in our lives, aiming to uncover the transformative power of this dynamic relationship. Givers, driven by their intuition and connectedness to the universe, embrace their responsibility to share their automatic downloads of wisdom, resources, and compassion. Receivers, equipped with the mental tools to effectively interpret and distribute this information, make a conscious choice to be open and receptive to their surroundings. Together, givers and receivers form a harmonious cycle where talents and performance are optimized, ultimately propelling humanity toward collective improvement and enhanced progress. Through personal anecdotes, psychological insights, and practical guidance, this book illuminates the potential for individuals to embrace their inherent roles as givers and receivers, unlocking the transformative power of their contributions for the betterment of humanity.

Understanding Unity and Oneness

The truth is: everything in the universe is formed from the same particles, from the largest stars to the inner workings of an atom. These particles are intricately interconnected and held together by an invisible and intelligent energy. As human beings, we are not exempt from this interconnectedness. In fact, as conscious beings, we are intimately connected to all of existence in ways we may not fully comprehend.

Consider this: each cell in our body holds a potential of 0.07 volts, and with approximately 50 trillion cells in an average body, we possess a staggering potential of 350 trillion volts. Our thoughts, intentions, words, and actions have a direct effect on the particles that form every cell within us. We are energetic beings, capable of influencing and shaping our reality.

Metaphorically, we are the center of our universe, with everyone and everything else serving as the stars and planets in our cosmos. Our intentions and actions ripple through this interconnected web, affecting not only ourselves but also the greater universe. Each choice we make, each word we speak, and each action we take has the power to create profound change, far beyond what we can imagine.

The Magnificent Hologram

In our quest to understand purpose, we must never forget that we are created in the image of a higher power. We are a hologram, a reflection of a much larger cosmic design. We carry within us the essence of the entire universe, and we should never take for granted the magnificent body and spirit we have been given to experience the wonders of life. In return, we have the power to co-create the universe we desire, to shape it with our intentions and actions.

Igniting the Inner Fire: The Power of the WHY Question

In the quest to unravel the essence of my being, a pivotal moment arrived when I dared to transform the very nature of my inquiries. No longer satisfied with the surface-level "what" and "who" questions, I delved deep into the heart of existence and embraced the transformative power of "Why."

Why, oh why, am I here in this vast tapestry of existence? Why do I possess these unique potentials that stir within me? Why is my soul driven to uncover the elusive enigma of purpose? And why, in this grand symphony of life, have I been granted the precious gift of existence?

These profound inquiries finally resonated within the depths of my being, igniting a fire of curiosity that burned brighter than ever before. They became the compass that guided me on an extraordinary journey of self-discovery, unveiling layers of truth and unlocking the hidden treasures of my soul. In embracing the power of "why," I ventured into the realms of the unknown, peering into the mysteries of the universe, and unearthing the profound purpose that lay dormant within.

As we explore the depths of purpose and our interconnectedness with the universe, we mustn't overlook the pivotal role of the "Why" question. It is this question that serves as the ignition for our inner fire, propelling us forward on our journey of self-discovery and transformation. The "Why" question holds within it the key to unlocking our true potential and aligning our actions with our deepest values.

When we ask ourselves, "*Why am I here, experiencing this physical life as a spiritual being?*" we tap into a wellspring of introspection and self-awareness. This question invites us to explore the essence of our existence, delve into the core of our being, and uncover the purpose that resides within us.

To embark on this journey of self-inquiry, we must be willing to embrace vulnerability and open our hearts to the whispers of our souls. It requires us to shed the layers of societal expectations and external validations, and instead, turn inward to listen to the wisdom that resides within us.

The process of seeking our purpose and understanding our place in the universe is not a linear path. It is a tapestry of experiences, insights, and revelations that weave together to form a profound understanding of our unique role in the grand symphony of life.

As we navigate this journey, it is essential to cultivate self-compassion and patience. Finding our purpose is not an overnight revelation but a gradual unfolding of our true selves. It requires us to embrace the twists and turns, the challenges and triumphs, and to remain steadfast in our commitment to seeking truth and authenticity.

Serving the Community and Humanity

In search of the answers to my "why" questions and armed with the knowledge gained from my journey and the practices I had developed, I felt a deep calling to serve my community and humanity at large. I recognized that the path to personal fulfillment was intricately tied to the well-being of those around me. As I embraced my purpose, I understood that true fulfillment is found not in isolation but in collective growth and support.

With this realization, I began offering guided visualization meditation sessions to my community. It was a humble effort to empower individuals, helping them tap into their inner fire and align their actions with their passions and purpose. Witnessing the transformation in the lives of others reaffirmed my conviction that embracing passion and purpose has the power to create a ripple effect of positive change.

The Birth of "Unity Meditation"

As my meditation practice deepened and I engaged with a growing community of seekers, a profound realization washed over me. It became evident that despite my initial assumptions, there were countless individuals harboring misconceptions about meditation and its boundless benefits. At that moment, the resounding answers to my "why" questions grew louder, compelling me to take action. It was time to share this transformative practice with the world.

Guided by intuition and fueled by my own experiences, I embarked on a mission to create a guided visualization meditation community. Within this sacred space, I carefully crafted meditation sessions that delved into fundamental aspects of life, intertwining them with the sublime power of sound vibrations and music. My intention was clear: to make meditation accessible and inviting for newcomers while igniting the flames of passion and purpose within every individual who embarked on this journey.

Through these immersive sessions, I witnessed firsthand the incredible transformation that visualization could bestow. Participants would immerse themselves in vibrant mental landscapes, exploring the depths of their dreams and embracing their most heartfelt desires. The once seemingly elusive practice of meditation suddenly became approachable and readily available, as barriers dissolved and limitless potential unfolded before their eyes. Within the sanctuary of these sessions, individuals shed the shackles of limiting beliefs, rediscovered their authentic selves, and emerged with a newfound sense of clarity and purpose.

The birth of Unity Meditation was the answer to one of my burning "why" questions—a revelation that we are here to serve one another and that our unique gifts emerge when we wholeheartedly share them. It became a movement of unity, where seekers joined forces, collectively harnessing the power of meditation to create positive ripples in their lives and the world. Together, we embarked on a journey of self-discovery and connection, embracing the truth that our paths are interwoven and that by uplifting one another, we amplify the light within ourselves.

Unity Meditation became a beacon of hope, illuminating the path toward self-realization and igniting a collective fire within the hearts of those who embarked on this transformative practice. It was a testament to the power of community, visualization, and the profound wisdom that lies within each of us. Through Unity Meditation, we embraced the boundless potential that resides within, and together, we embarked on a shared voyage of self-discovery and empowerment.

Conclusion

In the depths of our souls lies a longing for purpose, a yearning to ignite our inner fire and make a meaningful impact in the world. Through my personal experiences and reflections, I have come to realize that the search for purpose is a profound journey of self-discovery, unity, and understanding of our interconnectedness with the universe, and the flames of passion and purpose can lead to a life of fulfillment and meaningful impact, by shifting our focus from the individual "I" to the collective "we."

By embracing our passions, honoring our authentic selves, and asking the transformative "Why" question, we unlock the door to our inner fire. We tap into the vast potential that resides within us, realizing that we are co-creators of our reality and that our intentions and actions have the power to shape not only our lives but also the lives of those around us.

As you embark on your quest for purpose, I encourage you to delve deep into the recesses of your being, to listen to the whispers of your soul, and to embrace the unity and oneness that underlies all existence. May you find the answers you seek, and may your inner fire burn brightly, illuminating the path to a life filled with passion, purpose, and profound connection.

CHAPTER

Embracing Failure and
Discovering New Horizons
By Kyra Schaefer

Kyra Schaefer, CHI, is an accomplished Bestselling Author, Speaker, and dedicated Elevated Relationship and Emotional Wellness Coach. Boasting over two decades of expertise in Neuro-Linguistic Programming and Clinical Hypnotherapy, Kyra has garnered widespread acclaim for her role as a respected speaker and trainer. Through dynamic workshops and seminars, she shares her wealth of knowledge and experience, leaving a lasting impact on her audience.

Kyra's unyielding dedication to inspiring transformation is evident in every facet of her work. Whether she's empowering clients to conquer personal hurdles or delivering a captivating keynote address, her passion shines through. With Kyra's guidance, you can tap into your complete potential and attain the success you truly deserve.

Beyond her professional endeavors, Kyra's journey in martial arts, which commenced at the age of 14, has profoundly influenced her self-care approach. She imparts the power of this art form both privately and on stage, fostering growth in her clients and audiences alike, both in person and in virtual settings.

You can find her on her website at
https://www.kyra-schaefer.com/

YouTube Channel
https://www.youtube.com/@kyra-schaefer

Chapter 9

Embracing Failure and Discovering New Horizons

By Kyra Schaefer

Introduction

Have you ever felt paralyzed by the fear of trying something new? I know that feeling all too well. Deep within, I've always sensed that these new endeavors align with my true purpose, but that initial step can be overwhelmingly challenging. In this chapter, I'll share my personal journey as an entrepreneur, uncover the roots of my fear of failure, and explore the transformative power of learning from setbacks. I'll also introduce practical exercises and concepts that have helped me navigate the often tumultuous journey of pursuing my purpose through failure. So, join me on this journey of embracing failure to unlock the path to fulfilling your purpose.

My Journey as an Entrepreneur

Let me start by sharing my personal journey as an entrepreneur. Over time, I've birthed multiple businesses – some have achieved wild success, while others never quite got off the ground. My ventures have ranged from traditional brick-and-mortar stores to online platforms, from hobbies that felt like mere pastimes to make-or-break scenarios where failure would have meant destitution. Through it all, one belief has been my constant companion: everything happens for a reason and for my greater good.

This mindset shift was the first crucial step in my journey of embracing failure. Instead of viewing failure as a catastrophic endpoint, I learned to see it as part of a larger plan. Each setback became a stepping stone on my path to fulfilling my purpose. It's a powerful perspective shift that has enabled me to forge ahead despite the fear of failure.

Discerning Success and Failure

As I continued on my entrepreneurial journey, I developed the ability to discern which projects were destined for success and which would likely flounder.

After experiencing a few setbacks, I honed my ability to gauge whether my heart was genuinely invested in a project. Echoing John Maxwell's wisdom, "Fail fast, fail often, but always fail forward," I began to embrace failure as a constant companion. I learned to love the messy process of allowing my ideas to evolve organically. If a project was meant to flourish, it would find its wings; if not, well, there was always another venture in the pipeline.

This ability to discern the potential success of a project is a crucial skill in the journey toward fulfilling your purpose. It involves a deep understanding of your own passions, strengths, and values, which guide you in choosing endeavors that align with your true self. It's not about avoiding failure but rather about making more informed choices and learning from both successes and failures.

Failing Forward During the Pandemic

The COVID-19 pandemic presented me with a unique opportunity to explore new horizons. I decided to try new things, like learning to play the violin, even though I wasn't particularly successful – and I had to contend with some lingering hearing issues. I also picked up the ukulele and committed myself to daily painting sessions. My Qi Gong practice deepened, providing stability amidst the chaos. This period became an exhilarating experiment in continually failing at new pursuits. Along the way, I found myself achieving a modest level of proficiency in some of these endeavors.

The pandemic served as a global reminder that life is unpredictable and often throws us into unfamiliar territory. Embracing failure during these times of uncertainty is a powerful coping mechanism. It allows us to take risks, explore new passions, and adapt to changing circumstances. Even if these endeavors don't lead to immediate success, they contribute to personal growth and resilience.

Failure in the Learning Process

As an educator, I encountered students who were paralyzed by the fear of making mistakes. Whether it was painting, Qi Gong, Reiki, or Hypnosis training, the mere thought of imperfection led to self-condemnation. But isn't learning inherently about imperfection? Isn't "practice" precisely the process of honing skills through trial and error?

I often reassured my students, emphasizing that early attempts were merely practice runs. In the realm of Reiki, for instance, I stressed that energy itself guides the process, and perfection in hand placement isn't the goal. This highlights an important concept: the idea that failure is an integral part of the learning process. It's through our mistakes that we refine our skills, deepen our understanding, and ultimately reach a level of mastery.

The Roots of the Fear of Failure

"I am never upset for the reason I think." This principle from ACIM (A Course in Miracles) invites introspection. When emotions bubble up in response to potential failure, can we trace their origins back to their roots? Undoubtedly. The fear of failure often finds its roots in childhood, where perfection equated to receiving the love crucial for survival. Sometimes, we've traded genuine accomplishment for fleeting approval or pleasure. We've sought comfort in the approval we see in the eyes of others, but also felt the pain of their disapproval when we don't meet their standards.

This challenge isn't just about doing well in school or sports; it affects even basic things like doing chores properly or behaving as expected at family gatherings. Our early experiences with success and failure shape our beliefs and attitudes about ourselves and our abilities. Recognizing these patterns and understanding their origins is a critical step in overcoming the fear of failure. As you move forward allow yourself to begin to recognize that we are all worthy, loveable, whole and complete whether we "perform" perfectly or not.

Exercises: Deepening My Understanding

To help you explore and internalize the concepts discussed in this chapter, let's dive into a series of exercises and reflections. These exercises are designed to assist you in embracing failure as a pathway to fulfilling your purpose.

1. Reflective Journaling (Exercise): Write about a time when the fear of failure held you back from trying something new. What were the underlying thoughts and emotions? How did those feelings trace back to my past experiences?

2. Experiment with Imperfection (Exercise): Choose a creative activity such as drawing, painting, or playing an instrument. Purposefully create something imperfect and reflect on your feelings and thoughts during the process. How did it feel to let go of the need for perfection?

3. Mindful Failure Meditation (Exercise): Practice a guided meditation where you visualize embracing failure as a valuable teacher. Explore the emotions that arise during this visualization. How can you use these emotions to fuel your growth and purpose?

Embracing Failure in Pursuit of My Purpose

In 2023, I confronted unexpected fears when teaching Qi Gong and Asian-based movement practices in my community. Despite my extensive background in martial arts, doubts about cultural appropriation loomed large. I had been teaching Qi Gong and Falun Gong for years, combining philosophy, psychology, movement, and various therapeutic modalities. Nonetheless, the fear of misappropriation weighed on me.

Despite the fear, my heart's conviction prevailed, leading me to teach with authenticity and respect. The experience was enriching, as I shared ancient healing practices with attendees from diverse backgrounds at a recent "Celebrate Your Life" event in Stevenson, Washington. This event highlighted the importance of embracing failure when pursuing a higher purpose.

Overcoming such fears isn't easy. Our ego tends to grip us when navigating uncharted territories, whispering destructive narratives about impending disaster as we contemplate new paths. I, too, grappled with doubts and fears of backlash when teaching Qi Gong. I questioned my role and right to do so. Yet, the power of my purpose outweighed my fear. The outcome was gratifying, but what if it hadn't been? The key lies in testing and measuring.

The "Courageous Dream Manifestation Process"

The "Courageous Dream Manifestation Process" is a framework that I've developed to navigate the terrain of fear and uncertainty when pursuing a purpose-driven endeavor. This process involves several key components:

1. Confidential Sharing: Discuss my dream with close friends or trustworthy individuals who will offer positive support and encouragement. This step emphasizes the importance of seeking a supportive community when pursuing my purpose.

2. Professional Guidance: Seek mentors or coaches who can provide constructive feedback and hold me accountable. Mentorship can be invaluable in guiding me through the challenges of fulfilling my purpose.

3. Accountability Partners: Connect with an accountability partner who ensures my goals are met and exceeded. Having someone to share my progress and setbacks with can keep me on track.

4. Embracing Failure: Accept failure as a stepping stone to growth, learning, and redirection. This component emphasizes the central theme of this chapter – that failure is not the end but a valuable teacher.

5. Measurable Lessons: Recognize that failure is not a dead end but a source of knowledge, networking, and personal evolution. Each setback provides an opportunity to learn and refine my approach.

Through this process, I've come to understand that failure is a multifaceted gem, revealing layers of insight and self-discovery. While I've experienced profound success only a few times, I've forged connections that resonate at the core of my being. Embracing the prospect of failure and moving forward without hesitation holds the key to unlocking hidden potential and experiencing the beauty of life in its entirety.

Embracing Failure in the Creative Process

The creative process is inherently intertwined with the fear of failure. Whether you're an artist, writer, musician, or any form of creative thinker, the prospect of producing work that falls short of your vision can be paralyzing. However, I've come to understand that failure is an integral part of the creative journey and a powerful catalyst for artistic growth.

Artistic Endeavors and Creative Blocks

In my own creative endeavors, I've faced numerous creative blocks and periods of self-doubt. There were moments when I felt that my work was far from the vision I had in mind. These moments of perceived failure can be disheartening, leading to frustration and even a loss of motivation.

However, I've learned that creative blocks and imperfect work are not signs of failure but rather opportunities for experimentation and growth. Each so-called failure has pushed me to explore new techniques, perspectives, and styles. It's through these struggles that I've discovered my unique voice as a creative.

Writing, for instance, has been a constant source of both joy and frustration for me. There have been times when I've struggled to find the right words or convey my thoughts effectively. But these moments of writer's block have also led to breakthroughs in my writing, where I've uncovered fresh insights and developed a more authentic voice.

Failure as a Source of Innovation

In the world of innovation and entrepreneurship, failure is often celebrated as a necessary step toward success. Many groundbreaking inventions and technological advancements have emerged from a series of failures and iterations. I've come to appreciate that embracing failure in the creative process can lead to innovation and unexpected discoveries.

Consider the story of Thomas Edison and his quest to invent the electric light bulb. Edison famously said, "I have not failed. I've just found 10,000 ways that won't work." His relentless experimentation and willingness to embrace failure ultimately led to one of the most transformative inventions in history. It's a testament to the power of perseverance and the ability to view failure as a stepping stone rather than an obstacle.

In my own creative work, I've encountered numerous dead ends and discarded ideas. However, each failed attempt has propelled me forward, providing valuable insights and pushing me to explore uncharted territory. These moments of failure have been the catalysts for some of my most innovative and impactful creations.

Exercises: Embracing Failure in the Creative Process

Let's delve into exercises and reflections that can help us apply the concept of embracing failure in our creative endeavors and foster artistic growth:

1. Creative Block Exploration: Reflect on moments of creative block and self-doubt in your artistic pursuits. Write about how these challenges have ultimately contributed to your growth as a creative thinker.

2. Innovation and Iteration: Explore an area of your creative work where you've encountered failure and setbacks. Write about how these experiences led to innovation and unexpected discoveries. How can you continue to embrace failure as a source of creative growth?

3. Artistic Voice Discovery: Reflect on your artistic journey and how moments of failure have shaped your unique voice and style. Write about how you can further develop and express your creative identity.

4. Embracing Imperfection: Choose a creative project or piece of work that you consider imperfect. Write about how you can view this work as a valuable part of your creative evolution rather than a failure.

By engaging in these exercises, you'll not only embrace failure as an integral part of the creative process but also gain a deeper appreciation for how it can lead to artistic innovation and personal growth.

Embracing Failure as a Catalyst for Innovation

Innovation and entrepreneurship are domains where failure is not just common but often necessary for progress. I've come to understand that embracing failure in these realms is not a sign of weakness but a testament to one's willingness to take risks and push boundaries.

Entrepreneurial Ventures and Risk-Taking

As an entrepreneur, I've launched multiple businesses, some of which have flourished while others struggled or failed altogether. The entrepreneurial journey is inherently uncertain, and the fear of failure can be a constant companion. However, I've learned that it's precisely the willingness to take risks and embrace the possibility of failure that leads to innovation and growth.

In my entrepreneurial pursuits, I've encountered moments where it seemed like all was lost. Burnout, poor hiring choices, and unexpected obstacles threatened to derail my ventures. Yet, it was during these moments of crisis that I tapped into my creativity and resilience. I sought innovative solutions, pivoted when necessary, and emerged stronger and more adaptable.

One of the key lessons I've learned is that failure in entrepreneurship is not a reflection of one's worth or competence but a natural consequence of exploring uncharted territory. The ability to view these failures as opportunities for learning and adaptation is what sets successful entrepreneurs apart.

Failure as a Learning Opportunity

In the world of innovation, failure is not viewed as an endpoint but as a crucial part of the learning process. Each failed experiment, product iteration, or market pivot provides valuable data and insights that inform the next steps. I've applied this mindset in my entrepreneurial ventures, and it has allowed me to navigate uncertainty with greater confidence.

For instance, consider the world of technology startups. Many groundbreaking companies have emerged from a series of failures and pivots. These companies, including giants like Airbnb and Uber, started with different ideas and business models than what ultimately made them successful. Embracing failure as a form of rapid learning allowed them to adapt and respond to market dynamics.

In my own entrepreneurial journey, I've applied this principle by seeking feedback and conducting assessments after setbacks. Instead of dwelling on the failure itself, I focus on the lessons learned and how they can inform future endeavors. This approach has enabled me to innovate and iterate with greater agility.

Embracing Failure in Leadership and Personal Growth

Leadership is another arena where the fear of failure can be particularly paralyzing. The decisions leaders make have far-reaching consequences, and the fear of making the wrong choice can hinder progress. However, I've come to understand that embracing failure as a leader is essential for personal growth and organizational success.

Leadership and Decision-Making

In my role as a leader, I've faced numerous decisions that carried significant weight and uncertainty. The fear of making the wrong call, whether in business strategy or team management, was a constant presence. However, I've learned that leadership is not about avoiding failure but about making informed decisions and learning from the outcomes.

One of the key lessons I've internalized is that leaders who fear failure to the point of indecision often hinder progress and innovation within their organizations. The willingness to take calculated risks, make tough decisions, and accept the possibility of failure is what enables organizations to adapt and thrive in a dynamic world.

I've also discovered that transparent communication and vulnerability as a leader can be powerful tools for fostering trust and resilience within a team. By acknowledging the potential for failure and sharing the responsibility for outcomes, I've created an environment where team members feel empowered to take risks and contribute their ideas.

Failure as a Path to Personal Growth

Leadership and personal growth are intimately intertwined. As a leader, I've faced moments of self-doubt and imposter syndrome, wondering if I'm truly qualified to lead. These moments of perceived failure have led to profound personal growth and a deeper understanding of leadership itself.

In moments of leadership challenges, I've sought feedback from mentors, peers, and team members. I've embraced failure as an opportunity to refine my leadership style, enhance my emotional intelligence, and develop a greater capacity for empathy and adaptability. I've also recognized that leadership is not about being infallible but about continuous learning and improvement.

Conclusion: Embracing Failure as a Path to Fulfillment

Embracing failure is not a one-time endeavor but an ongoing journey that spans all aspects of our lives. Whether in our professional pursuits, personal growth, creative endeavors, innovation, or leadership roles, failure is a natural and necessary part of the path to fulfillment.

Through this chapter, I've shared my own journey of embracing failure and the valuable lessons I've learned along the way. I've explored the roots of the fear of failure, the transformative power of learning from setbacks, and practical exercises and concepts that can help us navigate the complex terrain of pursuing our purpose through failure.

I've also emphasized that failure is not a dead end but a stepping stone to growth, innovation, and personal development. It's a source of resilience, adaptability, and self-discovery. By reframing our relationship with failure and viewing it as a valuable teacher, we can unlock our hidden potential and experience the beauty of life in its entirety.

In closing, I encourage you to embark on your own journey of embracing failure. Whether you're pursuing a professional goal, seeking personal growth, nurturing your creative spirit, driving innovation, or leading others, remember that failure is not the enemy but a trusted companion on the path to fulfillment. Embrace it, learn from it, and let it propel you toward a life rich in purpose and meaning.

CHAPTER

Be Like a Five-Year-Old
By YuSon Shin

YuSon Shin is a gifted healer, intuitive, medium, speaker, author, and teacher of the healing and intuitive arts based in Los Angeles. With her trademark joyful and compassionate demeanor, she uses her gifts to help people and pets all over the world heal from a wide array of physical, emotional and spiritual ailments. YuSon loves teaching and holds workshops designed to help students awaken their own spiritual gifts and superpowers. She believes everyone has the power to heal themselves.

YuSon is an expert practitioner in a wide variety of healing techniques because she feels there is no "one size fits all" when working with her clients. She utilizes Akashic records and Chinese energy healing techniques to perform past life, karma and ancestral clearings. She is also a practitioner of the Bengston

Energy Healing Method and hosts the Los Angeles Bengston workshops. She is a certified Reiki Master, and also uses Integrated Energy Therapy, 5th Dimensional Quantum Healing, Quantum Touch, DNA Theta, and Access Bars. She is the author of six books, including, *Holistic*, *Manifestations*, *Whispers From The Heart*, *Soul Warrior*, *The Empath Effect*, *Be Bold* and *Ignite Your Inner Fire*.

You can reach YuSon at YuSon@ShinHealingArts.com and www.ShinHealingArts.com

Chapter 10

Be Like a Five-Year-Old

By YuSon Shin

Feeling stuck, empty, lost, frustrated, and unfulfilled is a familiar experience. These feelings arise when it's time for a growth spurt. Walking in shoes that I've outgrown can be painful. Even though I may have emotional attachments to the old shoes (representing old ways of being) and the joy and comfort they used to bring, I understand the necessity to size up. While the saying "When they go low, we go high" is effective when facing adversaries, during challenging times of personal growth and adulting, I go low. I lower my age by channeling a five-year-old. Not the five-year-old I used to be because I was painfully shy, but rather a charming, curious, and outgoing five-year-old like the kid in the movie *Jerry Maguire*. He makes friends with everyone, including a grown-up sports agent and shares interesting fun facts like "Did you know that the human head weighs eight pounds?"

When we feel lost in a cold, vast world, it makes sense to stoke the fire of our passion for the immediate benefit of warming ourselves with the flames of passion and purpose. When our levels of passion are high, it serves as a GPS for us to find and stay on the road to happiness and purpose. The secondary, less obvious, benefit is that our fires of passion also serve as a signal to others to find and support us. On a number of occasions, my passion for life had diminished to mere embers, requiring me to find ways to rekindle the flames and warm myself back to life. With experience, I've developed a process for leveling up and reigniting my inner fire, following a sensible order.

First, I start with clearing and preparing the area of the fire to prevent unwanted wildfires. This clearing process also serves as a reset for me. To start a fire without clearing first is like starting a fire on an emotional hazardous waste site. I check myself so I don't wreck myself. Depending on the severity of the situation, I engage in activities like dousing myself with holy water or immersing myself in a satisfying sound bath to cleanse and bless my space. This may look to the outside world like crying and screaming into a pillow and have varying degrees of emotional output. I have found that it is so satisfying to go all out and to do it like a five-year-old throws a good old-fashioned tantrum that can only be described as a full meltdown in the privacy of my own home because a good clearing shouldn't get other people dirty. Energy clearings are respectable and respectful. Kids do it best when they have an honest cry and then move on. By feeling and releasing my emotions instead of suppressing them, I establish a better foundation for building the next segment of my future.

In addition to the dramatic tantrum technique, these other techniques can help us reset and break free from old thoughts, patterns, and habits that have been developed through routine or the trauma of survival. These techniques may appear less dramatic but are equally effective in creating fresh starts:

1. Vacation: Stepping away from your regular environment and routine can provide a much-needed break and perspective. It allows you to explore new places, cultures, and experiences, opening your mind to different possibilities. I recently used this reset. After about ten years of working both a corporate job and a full-time healing business, I decided to quit my corporate career. The end of my corporate job coincidentally timed perfectly with a trip to Egypt that was preplanned. I took the time to release the stress of working two full-time jobs

for a decade and allowed myself to daydream about how I wanted my business to feel and look going forward. Vacations allow you to play and reinvent yourself because no one knows you. As I do on most vacations, the inner kid in me waved to everyone from the tour bus and said hello to as many people as I could using new Arabic phrases learned. I made an effort to remember people's names which made them feel special. The tour bus drivers, security guards, and guides were blown away because most tourists don't even bother to ask their names or ask how they are doing. Because of the trip, I reaffirmed my desire to help people and knew that I wanted to design my business to be international, and I wanted to integrate travel into my life.

2. Volunteer: Engaging in volunteer work can shift your focus from your problems to the needs of others. It helps you develop empathy, gratitude, and a broader perspective on life. Volunteering exposes you to new ideas, people, and situations, stimulating personal growth and igniting inspiration. When I was younger, I had more time than money, so I set out to teach illiterate adults to read. I was assigned an ex-con who was living in a halfway house. He aspired to be

a short-order cook in a restaurant, and I would not have gotten to know his story if I hadn't volunteered.

3. Engaging with new people: Actively seeking conversations with people in areas of interest or new social circles can expand your horizons. By engaging in meaningful conversations and connecting with individuals who share your passions or goals, you can gain fresh insights and new perspectives. There is a saying, "You are the average of the five people you spend the most time with." Boost your average with inspirational and interesting new friends. When I don't want to invest too much time or money on something, I find someone who is already doing it, and I ask what they like and dislike about it. After I graduated from UCLA, I had already been putting myself through college doing paralegal work and wondered if going to law school was the next step for me. I knew that I didn't want to incur student loan debt only to find out I didn't love it, so I reached out to all the lawyers I could access to ask as many questions as I could. I concluded after interviewing many attorneys that law school was not what I wanted.

4. Get physical: Physical activity is a powerful way to reset and reconnect with yourself. Engag-

ing in any form of movement helps release stress, boosts endorphins, and enhances overall well-being. It brings you into the present moment, allowing you to focus on the sensations in your body and clearing your mind of clutter.

5. Meditation (Still and Walking): Practicing meditation provides a valuable opportunity to quiet the mind, let go of racing thoughts, and find inner stillness. By dedicating time to be in silence and observing your thoughts without judgment, you can create space for clarity, introspection, and renewed energy.

Resetting allows you to open yourself up to new possibilities. It's like becoming a blank canvas once again, ready to paint a new picture of your life.

Next, after clearing the area, is to find some kindling for your fire. Find what lights you up, makes your toes curl with excitement, and will motivate you enough to keep you going despite hardships. Sometimes that means taking inventory of what you already enjoy. If you are unsure and want insight into your subconscious desires, look into what you talk about most or spend your time and money on. What are your strengths? What fills you up? What do you find meaningful or fulfilling? What have you wanted to try? I was surprised to notice that for more than a decade, I chose to invest my money and time in healing classes more than any other activity.

Getting clarity on our preferences may require us to reevaluate existing truths. At some point, we adopted the preferences of our parents and friends, and we mistook them for ours. Maybe we were always served scrambled eggs growing up but having eggs benedict has shifted our preference for poached eggs. As time passes, our tastes also evolve and change. Our most recent experiences also give us opportunities to evaluate. Every time I ended a job or relationship, I took inventory of qualities I would like to have in the next and what I would like to shift. Take time to rediscover preferences, identify what does and doesn't work, and explore the things that bring joy. By being like a five-year-old who questions everything and is driven by endless energy, we can revisit our preferences and passions, which then refuel our dreams.

Kids say what they want out loud and share their desires with whoever will listen. They can unapologetically wish for the moon. They decide based on how they feel in the moment and do not hesitate to choose something different without judgment. Kids don't judge themselves for changing their minds. They don't mind reaching for something better or different. Adults are afraid to want, much less declare it to the world for fear of disappointment.

We can take a page from kids who effortlessly make friends simply by saying "Hi." They are open to play and change, with their personalities still developing and identities yet to solidify. At that age, they can be anything they want, and the world is their playground. As adults, we often struggle with rigidity in our thoughts and lives, finding it challenging to make new friends when our existing friends move away. We need reminders to play and let go of attachments to permanence. Adults often fear change and cling to decisions, feeling obligated to stay the course as if everything were written in stone. We even stop dreaming, which results in feeling the pain of unfulfilled aspirations or the pain of regret from not taking action. Children, on the other hand, can shift directions when something isn't working. Mastery of the monkey bars has taught them that to move forward, they need to let go of the rung behind them to grab the next to move forward. Reaching for the next rung is a growth move, meaning bigger and more comfortable shoes are coming to accommodate my growth spurt.

Life is about having meaningful experiences, and not all have to be successful. The best learning experiences can come from our failures and pain. Pain on the monkey bars of life comes from our inability to let go of the bar behind us. For years, I struggled and hung without momentum on the bars when trying to keep my healing and psychic abilities a secret as I was working in the corporate world. It was painful to let my fears deceive me into believing I could be successful while I was still in the closet. I came to realize that one grows into the space given, and the closet is a very small space. After I proudly let my co-workers know what I was passionate about, I could also tell the world, and then my healing business grew.

My next growth spurt happened again when I realized that the next rung on the monkey bars meant I had to give up my corporate career to feel truly happy. My metaphoric hands were raw as I hung painfully between the energy healing which I love, and the corporate world which paid me a regular salary that gave me a huge sense of security. I swung my legs for momentum and let go of the rung that represented the corporate world. I reached for and got a good handle on the next rung, which was to grow my business even bigger. I'm always happy with the growth from the momentum, which means I can wear a bigger shoe size.

Third, learn to shield your fire from the winds of negativity, even your own. Break down your fears. Fear of failing. Fear of rejection. Fear that you are just too young, too old, too broke. And I stopped talking to people who weren't supportive. Instead, I invite my most supportive friends to come to cheer me on while I'm on the monkey bars. I don't engage the naysayers who tell me that mastering the monkey bars is too dangerous or there is no point.

Before my career transition at the ripe age of 54, these success stories bolstered my resolve to keep going whenever I felt too old and too scared to change. Stephen Spielberg was rejected from film school three times. Vincent Van Gogh only sold one painting while he was alive for a very small amount of money. It blows my mind that Walt Disney was fired from one of his first animation jobs because he "lacked imagination and had no good ideas." Zoom was founded by Eric Yuan at the age of 41. Sam Walton founded Walmart at 44. Julia Child published her first cookbook at 50. Louise Hay started Hay House Publishing at 61. Colonel Harlan Sanders established Kentucky Fried Chicken at 62 and began franchising at 65.

For those of you who fear you are too young, here are success stories of the very young. Bill Gates and Mark Zuckerberg founded Microsoft and Facebook, respectively, at the young age of 19. And here are examples of uber-successful people who came from nothing. Oprah Winfrey grew up in poverty in rural Mississippi. Steve Jobs, co-founder of Apple, was given up for adoption, and his adoptive parents struggled financially. Larry Ellison of Oracle dropped out of college twice due to financial constraints, and J.K. Rowling of the

Harry Potter series of books was a single mother living on welfare.

Understanding the different archetypes and their corresponding resistance points can help individuals in pursuing their passions. Let's explore each archetype and the strategies that can be useful for each:

1. Interested About Everything. This archetype represents individuals who have a wide range of interests and passions. They may find themselves constantly drawn to new ideas and experiences, making it challenging to focus on a single path. To overcome the resistance of being overwhelmed by too many options, it is recommended for this archetype to clear the areas where they are building their fires of passion, as they have a high probability of creating wildfires. This means taking the time to reflect, filter, and prioritize their interests. By creating a clear space and narrowing down their focus, they can avoid spreading themselves too thin and allow themselves to make meaningful progress in their chosen area of passion.

2. Completely Lost. This archetype represents individuals who feel lost and unsure about their passions and purpose in life. They may struggle to identify a single area of interest or feel

overwhelmed by the lack of clarity. For this archetype, the focus should be on finding kindling. This involves exploring various activities, experiences, and interests to discover what resonates with them. Engaging in self-reflection, trying new things, and seeking inspiration from others can help in uncovering hidden passions. Individuals in this archetype need to be patient with themselves and embrace the process of exploration and self-discovery.

3. Procrastinator. This archetype represents individuals who may struggle with discipline, motivation or experience overwhelm. They may find it challenging to take action on their passions and often delay or avoid pursuing their goals, only to be saddled with regret. For this archetype, the key focus is on shielding your flames of passion from negativity and surrounding yourself with supportive friends. Creating a positive and encouraging environment can help boost motivation and provide accountability. Seeking the support of friends who believe in their potential and can offer encouragement and guidance can be instrumental in overcoming procrastination tendencies. Developing effective time management skills, setting realistic goals, and breaking tasks into smaller, man-

ageable steps can also aid in overcoming overwhelm and taking consistent action.

In summary, it's never too late to embrace the wisdom of a five-year-old and embark on a journey of self-discovery and personal growth. Reach for the next monkey bar. Remember the basic steps:

1. Clear your space before you build your fire of passion and purpose. The Interested About Everything Archetype should focus on this step.

2. Find kindling. Know what you want. Know what you like. This is an area that needs extra attention for the Completely Lost Archetype.

3. Shield your fire from the winds of negativity. The Procrastinator Archetype's weakness can be counteracted with this step.

CHAPTER Eleven

Living The Dream
By Janice Story

Meet Janice Story, an Equine Assisted Coach who has found healing and inspiration through her connection with horses. Janice is a Certified Reiki Master/Teacher, Certified Animal Reiki Practitioner, Certified Mind, Body, Spirit Practitioner, and The Shipp Method Christ Centered Trauma Recovery Certified professional. She is also an Author, Public Speaker, Ordained Minister, and Yoga Nidra Facilitator.

Janice's unique approach to healing merges equine-assisted coaching with other facets of her expertise. Her deep affinity with horses has played a crucial role in her personal healing journey, and she now harnesses this bond to guide her clients toward accessing their innate wisdom and healing abilities.

Utilizing the silent language and calming presence of her horses, Janice creates a safe environment for her clients to experience, articulate, release, and ultimately transform their pain and trauma.

Her gentle, compassionate nature fosters a nurturing and supportive space for clients to delve into their emotions and openly express themselves. The powerful connection she shares with horses enhances her healing practice, as the unspoken communication and presence of these magical companions can facilitate transformative experiences beyond those achievable through human interaction alone.

Janice provides private and group sessions, workshops, and trainings at her serene sacred sanctuary. She is also the co-founder of The Freedom Way Equine Assisted Coaching Certification program, empowering individuals to become certified Equine Assisted Coaches. Additionally, Janice is a valued team member at Soberman's Estate, serving as an Equine and Meditation Coach.

www.Janicestory.com

janice.story@me.com

Chapter 11

Living the Dream

By Janice Story

As I sat down to write this story a week ago, I wasn't sure where I would begin, as I have been on such an incredible journey over the last thirteen years. My head was full of thoughts and ideas about the experiences I wanted to share, but the words wouldn't come out. As I sit here today writing now, I realize it was because the dream I am currently in the middle of needed to be part of this story. I am writing this from The Sacred Valley in Peru, in the middle of what seems like a dream, truly living my best life. The years of learning how to find and ignite my inner fire have led me to an incredible experience. Now, how did I get here?

Has there ever been a moment in your life when you stopped in your tracks and asked yourself, 'What is the meaning of all this?' 'What is the purpose of my existence?' Do you ever feel as though you're merely existing, rather than truly living, as if your life lacks the vibrancy and meaning it once had? Do you find yourself questioning the monotony of your existence, wondering, 'Isn't there more to life than this?' I can confidently say I've been there, having spent a good part of my last ten years in corporate America grappling with these and many more questions.

I dedicated two and a half decades of my life to the corporate retail world. I don't deny that there were moments of joy and satisfaction. There was a time when it was genuinely fulfilling and I enjoyed my job. However, circumstances change, and businesses often lose sight of what truly matters—their people, and it's easy to become entrapped in a vicious cycle of negativity and disillusionment.

These persistent questions swirling in my thoughts started me on a journey to rediscover and reconnect with my own self, and embrace my authenticity. The quest was to understand who I truly was once more, as I had somehow lost sight of my identity in the bustle, chaos, and trauma of life. We're called 'human beings,' but it feels like we have morphed into 'human doings,' more concerned with action than existence.

Just as I began my journey, my life took an unexpected tumultuous turn, plunging me into the depths of complex PTSD and compelling me to confront over forty years of unprocessed trauma. In March 2010, I bore witness to a horrific incident resulting in four fatalities and five critically injured people. The specifics of the incident need not be shared here, but its aftermath thrust all the pent-up trauma from my past to the surface, occupying my every waking moment. I was plagued by sleepless nights, haunted by memories of past emotional, physical and sexual abuse, loss, grief, abandonment, and more. All my past pains, which I had carefully compartmentalized and sealed away, were now scattered around me, as if a tornado had ripped open the locked boxes of my past. I describe PTSD as a video that plays on an endless loop, in high definition, full color, sounds, tastes, and smells, and you cannot find the remote.

I found myself lost and confused, unable to comprehend the tumult of emotions and the condition I was in. As a survivor, I had always conquered whatever challenges or hurdles life had thrown at me, no matter their magnitude. But now, I found myself in uncharted territory, coming to terms with the fact that, for once, I needed assistance, that I needed to reach out, and that I needed to learn to accept and welcome support from others. I won't dive into the details of my traumatic past, as it is now behind me. Instead, I aim to inspire you, to assure you that regardless of life's trials and tribulations, you have the power to ascend. You have the ability to realize your dreams and achieve your highest aspirations.

There's a saying, 'When the student is ready, the teacher appears,' and my journey stands as a testament to this. In some inexplicable way, I was divinely steered toward the right individuals who supported my healing process. It hasn't been a smooth ride, but today, I genuinely appreciate all of life's experiences, particularly the challenging ones. That was a pivotal lesson I learned from one of my guides. Sunny Dawn Johnston taught me to seek and appreciate the lessons ingrained in my experiences. You might wonder how I could possibly extract value from the traumatic 2010 accident, but it was indirectly because of it that I encountered Sunny.

Sunny, along with numerous others, has journeyed with me, at times leading the way and at others merely accompanying me. They taught me to accept my past rather than perpetually evading the pain associated with it. I learned to truly experience my emotions and realized it was safe to do so, which ultimately led to healing. I no longer carry the weight of shame, fear, or sadness, as they no longer serve a purpose in my life. Clinging on to the past hindered my capacity to live in the present moment, to cherish my life. Adapting to this change wasn't easy. Indeed, it was a demanding endeavor, but the outcome of learning to let go was a liberating sensation of freedom.

One invaluable technique I picked up was to chronicle my thoughts and emotions, providing an outlet for my cluttered mind. Through this act of journaling, I began to uncover forgotten fragments of myself. I found myself revisiting interests and activities I had once enjoyed but had dismissed as unrealistic or trivial, under the notion that they could not be translated into a successful livelihood. Journaling was a practice of introspection that enabled me to delve deep into the recesses of my life's experiences, my yearnings, and my passions. During one such relative session, I came to the realization that I needed to reintegrate my passion for horses into my professional life. Horses had always been a central part of my existence—I had previously trained thoroughbred racehorses. The challenge now was to find a way to combine this consuming passion with a rewarding and successful career.

While juggling my duties as a retail store manager, I evolved into a Reiki Master and a life coach, and began working with clients, yet I never believed this could offer me stability. I continued to see clients, and when I brought my horses into my client sessions, I witnessed moments of profound healing. This led me to recognize that this was my true passion and life's calling. However, the question, 'How could I bring this dream to fruition?' felt unanswerable. Despite the difficulties in my corporate role, it guaranteed security for my family. How could I possibly detach myself from that?

My passion for the horses had lain dormant within me, wanting to be rediscovered. It was as if I had been a piece of a jigsaw puzzle, and I had finally found where I fit. All I needed to determine now were the specifics—the how, when, and where. As I maintained my journaling practice, I found myself illustrating the sensation of partnering with horses. I was exposed to various healing techniques, such as visualization and meditation. I began to imagine myself engaging with clients, conversing with them, even witnessing them interacting with a specific horse of mine. Sometimes, I would even assign them names. I employed meditation to affirm my intention of leaving my job to chase my dreams.

Clients did start trickling in, and over the ensuing years, my life began to transform. I was literally attracting remarkable things into my life. However, it wasn't an overnight journey, and my healing process, while necessary, was exhaustive. I felt like I was on a rollercoaster, oscillating between being trapped in the past and advancing in the right direction. I would momentarily surrender to trust and faith, only to quickly relapse into fear. It was challenging to maintain a steady course. All the while, I was still clocking in sixty to seventy hours a week in my retail position and attending to clients during nights and weekends. This relentless schedule began to take its toll on me, and I started neglecting my own self-care.

During a session with Sunny, she highlighted my current neglect of self-care, aiding me in recognizing that it was time for a change. She helped me understand that as long as I straddled the divide between my corporate job and my true passion, I was inhibiting my progress. I had to grasp the fact that the door I yearned to open would only do so once I was ready to firmly shut the other. What an epiphany that was! When I shared my thoughts about stepping down to a different position at work, she promptly asked, "When?" After a moment's consideration, I impulsively responded, "Sometime this fall." Given that it was only January, the fall seemed like a safe bet, providing ample time to figure things out.

I initiated discussions with my husband, Kent, about the changes I wished to implement. A few years earlier, we had converted a section of our deck into a remarkable healing room, one of my previously mentioned manifestations. There it was—I already had this fantastic space where I conducted a few Reiki classes along with client sessions. Perhaps, there was a chance I could make this truly work. Kent was well aware of my growing dissatisfaction with my job, and we both had reservations about whether I could generate sufficient income to make it viable. As we deliberated, he expressed his support for my decisions, and I commenced the process of solidifying my plan.

As the months of 2018 swiftly rolled by and fall neared, a hint of nervousness began to creep in, coupled with an undercurrent of fear. Was I genuinely prepared to take this leap? My plan to step down seemed like a safety net, allowing me to work three ten-hour days while maintaining my insurance. That felt less risky than diving headfirst into retirement! But the question remained: would I be able to draw in enough clients to compensate for the drop in income?

I think it was around late July when Kent came home from a town council meeting. They were planning to establish a men's residential treatment center in our neighborhood. Initially, I was apprehensive about this development in our locality. However, my interest was piqued when he showed me their plans for the therapeutic practice to be included. He pointed out equine therapy on the list and suggested, "Why don't you call them?" I immediately dismissed the idea, thinking they would never hire me as they'd likely be looking for a licensed therapist. I believed I wouldn't even make the shortlist. He retorted, "Just call them. What harm could it do, right?"

After a few days of gathering my courage, I eventually scheduled a meeting with Mitch Prager, the owner and founder of Soberman's Estate. We spent around an hour and a half at a local Starbucks, during which I shared about myself and my passion for working with horses. I also mentioned my practice as a mind, body, spirit practitioner and later circled back to this point. We discussed the importance of treating the whole body and had a truly engaged conversation. He informed me that they wouldn't be ready to open until November and were just starting the interview process, promising to contact me in October.

Although Mitch didn't hire me immediately, I was determined that I would work with him. My plan was underway and the wheels were in motion. I started sharing with everyone that I'd be stepping down in November because I was going to work at Soberman's Estate. During my journaling sessions, I found myself returning to writing—as I'd mentioned earlier—about working with the men who would be clients at Soberman's. I would assign them names and visualize myself facilitating equine experiences with them. As these visualizations grew stronger, I felt an unwavering belief that I was about to manifest my dream job!

When October rolled around, I conversed with Mitch once more. He informed me that the opening was postponed until January 2019 and that he'd reach out then, still without hiring me. Undeterred, I stuck to my plan and, despite some apprehension, took the plunge and stepped down. I was now working three days a week, allowing me to attend to more of my own clients at home.

The call finally came in early March 2019 from Mitch, presenting me with the opportunity to become the Equine and Meditation coach at this prestigious luxury treatment center for professional men battling alcohol and substance addiction. Astonishingly, I'd manifested my dream job right in my backyard. Overlooking the fact that I hadn't mentioned the location earlier, the center was so close I could either walk or ride my horses to work, with just about four hundred steps separating my back gate from the barn within this stunning property. Was this real? Could it truly be happening?

I started my job at Soberman's on my days off from the retail world, and in the meantime, my creative gears shifted into overdrive. Reaching out to a cherished friend, Diana Gogan, we co-founded 'The Freedom Way,' a certification course for equine-assisted coaching. Diana echoed my enthusiasm for letting horses take center stage in this coaching approach rather than merely being tools within a pre-determined, scripted session. We would hold our first class in the spring of 2020. So there I was, finally unearthing my true passion: serving others.

The years 2019 and 2020 brought trials and tribulations for many. Amidst the universal chaos, I felt a twinge of guilt at the blessings that poured into my life. As fear of contagion made public spaces less appealing, people started reaching out to me for guidance, comforted by the natural expansion of our ranch. It became apparent that it was time for me to sever the ties with my corporate life. It was time for me to fully step into trust and take that leap of faith. Thus, after a twenty-four-year journey, I bid goodbye to the corporate world at the end of 2020. Almost immediately, three new clients reached out to me. It was as if the door didn't just open, but was flung wide as if welcoming me into my new life.

For more than four years now, I've had the honor of engaging with the remarkable men at Soberman's. Each week, I lead three equine sessions, one meditation session, and two group sessions. To call it 'work' seems almost unfair, as it is more of a calling. When you discover your passion, it seamlessly integrates into your life. Each morning brings a new sense of purpose and enthusiasm, as the customary work-related stress fades away. It's a life filled with meaning, purpose, and anticipation for each new day.

In the span of roughly six years, I've contributed to seven collaborative book projects, hosted numerous events at my ranch, and launched two thriving businesses of my own. I've also had the privilege of conducting equine workshops for Celebrate Your Life. Still actively working with clients and teaching various classes, I am constantly seeking avenues to support others on their unique journeys. It's hard to envision where I'd be today if it wasn't for the tiny spark, years ago, that kindled my passion and nudged me towards becoming my authentic self.

The happiness that I derive from my work every day is beyond anything that I have ever experienced from the walls of the corporate world I once lived in. Every day is different and meaningful. I feel a strong sense of purpose that has given meaning to my existence. This newfound passion brought with it a deep sense of satisfaction, giving me the feeling of truly being alive. Each morning, I wake up with an eagerness to make a difference, to contribute to a cause larger than myself. It's a life that is far removed from my previous existence, but one that feels profoundly right.

So, here I am, on a once-in-a-lifetime trip to Peru, something I never would have dreamed I could have ever done. It feels like I am in another universe and so surreal as I sit here writing, thinking about my life and how far I have come. I have reconnected with myself, and for the first time in my life, I can say that I love who I have become, and I am proud of myself and all that I've accomplished in life. I feel so much gratitude for all that I have attracted into my life, and I know that you can do the same! You are so worthy and deserving of great things. Don't ever let fear hold you back from chasing your own dreams.

I have found my purpose, the thing that set my heart on fire. I've discovered that I was not just a tiny speck in the universe, but a vital part of it, with a meaningful role to play. I found that my purpose in life was not something that was assigned to me, but something that I discovered within myself. And in finding my purpose, I found my joy, my peace, and my happiness.

My aspiration is that my journey will inspire you to embark on your own path of healing and transformation. May you rekindle the connection with your inner self and step boldly into your authenticity. I hope that you can light your personal spark and unveil your true passion. May you trust your inner compass, guiding you towards a life brimming with adventure and joy. Remember, you hold the pen. You possess the paper—you are the writer of your own narrative. Make it an exceptional one!

CHAPTER

Twelve

This Journey We Call Life
By Chantalle Ullett

Chantalle Ullett, a native French Canadian, is a highly skilled practitioner dedicated to holistic healing. As a Licensed Massage Therapist, Certified Bodytalk Practitioner, Certified Hypnotherapist, and Life Coach, she offers a range of modalities to treat the body, mind, and spirit.

Chantalle's unique approach encompasses various techniques, including Linking Awareness, which fosters heartfelt connections with sentient beings, and the Bodytalk System, which addresses the complete well-being of individuals. Her extensive travels have allowed her to witness the transformative power of healing, not only in humans but also in animals such as horses, cats, dogs, orangutans, elephants, and dolphins.

During sessions, Chantalle combines integrative approaches, advanced breathwork techniques, and advanced bodywork modalities to achieve lasting results. Her practice is located in the NW Suburbs of Chicago, where she continues her personal healing journey.

To benefit from Chantalle's expertise, you can reach her at chantalleullett@gmail.com or (815) 403-9106. Remember, life offers numerous paths, and Chantalle is here to guide you toward a fulfilling and transformative adventure.

Chapter 12

This Journey We Call Life

By Chantalle Ullett

Here I am, sitting under an old majestic oak tree by the dam close to my house. Observing the Canadian geese mingling with others from their flock on the water, the white mystical crane simply hangs out by the rolling water flowing downstream from the dam. Seagulls flying high in the sky without a care in the world and the wondrous cormorants sunbathing on the island in the trees on the small island across from me. The ants are busy traveling across my bare feet, which are nestled in the grass in front of me, just as I am embraced by a light breeze blowing the hot air, pondering what my purpose in life is. You see, it is very easy to get lost in oneself and the problems/tribulations we think we have. It also sucks the life and energy out of you when you're an overthinker, such as myself.

It isn't as though I want to overthink every little aspect of life, but there are times when I am utterly consumed. Spiraling down a vicious, dark, damp rabbit hole. You know the one, I'm sure of it. Take, for example, you are at work, and all of a sudden, your boss tells you they want to talk to you but do not expand any further. For me, this situation is terrifying. It used to bring me back to a time when I was younger, struggling academically in school, always being told I wasn't smart enough, lazy, no good or consistently being compared to my sibling, who was extremely academically inclined. So instead of taking a deep conscious breath to calm myself, my ego mind takes over. Playing out a variety of scenes, from "I'm doing a lousy job" to "Why can't I be more efficient," however, most scenes involve me being let go.

This is just the beginning. Seems to be a silly concept, but it's true. We go through many moments which seem more poignant than others. Most of these moments go back to my childhood. Our childhood is extremely impactful, at least for me. Perhaps for you too? We have all sorts of memories, good, bad, amazing, unforgettable, and terrifying, as well as some which can feel soul-crushing. I've spent a good portion of my life in various modes. All the while learning, growing, and healing. At the tender age of 50, you'd think I would have it figured out. Nope, not this one.

Webster defines the meaning of purpose as "something set up as an object or end to be obtained."

A friend asked me as I decided to write this story for this book, what are the three most heartrending *things* I learned at the different times of my life when I didn't feel I had purpose or passion in my life? After much reflection, the first purpose of my life was simply to *survive* and *cope* with having to depend solely on myself. This goes way back to my childhood. Remember when I said we have good, bad, soul-crushing memories? I grew up in a dysfunctional family, as most of society has, I think. Having moved around a lot as a child, attending multiple schools in different cities, I struggled academically, was bullied, didn't fit in anywhere, and didn't have many friends. It wasn't until I was 27 years old I finally told my parents about the variety of abuse I endured at the hands of family members. This was met with disbelief upon hearing. Eventually, in time, many years later, it was met with what I believe: understanding. As I am writing this, my whole body is shaking with anxiety. Not because I am ashamed or feel guilty but because my family doesn't want anyone else to know. Why? Because no one else needs to know; it's one of those family secrets. It has taken me over 47 years to build a bond with my mom. I'm not honestly sure how she will react once she reads this.

I was 5 years old, on a frigid, blizzardy night. My sibling and I were in our shared bed, about to fall asleep. Our Doberman, Duke, was sound asleep at the end of the bed on top of our warm blanket. My nightly ritual consisted of hugging Duke before laying my head down. My sibling, who wasn't fond of dogs or me, knew my nightly routine, purposely yanking the blanket under our dog as I was giving him his nightly kiss. Everything after that happened in a flash, as they say. Duke was startled and did what any animal would do; he bit. The unfortunate part was it was my left eye. Events are somewhat blurry. I remember being in the car on the way to the hospital, getting stuck in a snowbank, then on a table with all these people in white hovering over me while I cried out for my parents. Some would say it was purely an accident. However, moments like this with my sibling were not uncommon.

The mental/verbal/emotional abuse was constant for a few decades. My sibling enjoyed tormenting me everywhere. At home, school, and lying to my parents, my friends, mutual friends or extended family, and my partners. When I was 16, we got into yet another argument, this time over control of the remote for the TV. Their partner was over, and somehow they decided to get involved, threatening to come after me. Needless to say, I didn't back down. I wrote my dad a letter saying I was not going to come home if they were still there. Yet again, they had managed to talk their way out of the situation, and I was blamed yet again.

The sexual abuse I endured happened at the hands of two people in my life. I was fairly young. About 5 years old. I truly didn't understand it was sexual abuse until I was sitting in my counselor's office discussing what I was convinced was my doing. I was brainwashed to think I was the one asking for it, to play the games, to enact scenarios. Years later, when I was 17, my boyfriend thought he could have sex with me whether I consented or not.

I suffered from depression a lot during my adolescence, thoughts of suicide were prevalent, and I attempted to commit suicide once. Thankfully a friend stopped me. I didn't understand what anxiety was. I was just on edge all of the time. I was extremely negative, resentful, and worried. I had difficulties speaking to anyone. I was dismissed at every turn. The worst of it all was the soul-crushing aspect of my life. I just wanted someone, anyone, to love me for me. In all of this, I knew there had to be more to life I was meant to do, be more despite my circumstances.

The second purpose in my life was to learn how to *heal* and *move forward* in life. This proved to be more challenging. Why, you might ask? It seems as though it would be easy to do or overcome, but a person such as myself, I had to first understand the concept that life is a journey that affects the entirety of one's being. At times, I wish I had realized this earlier in my life as it would've made the transition of who I am much easier to understand and deal with. Less frustration, fewer struggles, less overthinking, for sure. Maybe even fewer trips to the doctor(s). However, I've also been shown by the creator, universe, and divine everything happens when it's supposed to. You can't rush *anything*.

This was instrumental in the second part of my purpose. The *healing* aspect was and still is instrumental. As it has to happen on all levels; mental, physical, and spiritual. For if one is out of balance, all are out of balance on some level. How we choose to address our path to healing varies for everyone.

For me, I started with the physical, as this was all I knew in the beginning. Then as time went on, the merging of mental awareness. Less than two decades ago, the weaving of spiritual healing came.

Let me explain what I mean. As most people do, we go to the doctor and explain our symptoms, pains, and aches; the doctors, in turn, prescribe medications or some form of treatment plan. I continued with this very exhausting ritual for many years. Sometimes my physical pain and aches would go away. The pills my doctor gave me for my depression and anxiety helped curb the roller coaster ride of my emotions and moods I dealt with on a daily basis. Yet I still felt as though something was off. My health didn't really improve, my mental state of being wasn't as jovial as you would think, and my whole demeanor was in a state of numbness. My doctor suggested I speak with a counselor to discuss the depression and anxiety I was dealing with. So I did. Well, let's say the first counselor I saw nailed my issues right off the bat. However, I was not in a mental state of acceptance to hear what he said. He told me to move out of my parents' house as well as not be in a relationship with anyone. That was almost 30 years ago.

It took another 10 years for me to actually seek out another counselor, continuing on with my journey of self-healing. I also sought out more natural ways to help heal my mental state, as I didn't want to continue with pills. Yes, they help for a while to even out my mood and lessen the roller coaster ride of emotions I felt. But there had to be more. A more natural way of dealing with the pain. My choice to go back to school opened the door to alternative therapies I would not have ever considered. It also helped me discover my passion in life which is to help people heal from their own traumas and pains. There have been many energetic modalities that have contributed to my process. Some of the sessions I have received were Bodytalk, Reiki, massage, myofascial release, and a variety of energetic sessions which cannot be put into words. I even had a session with a practitioner who used live bees. That was fascinating. I lay on the table, and he would first ask the bees which one wanted to be of service to me. Then he would grab the bee, thank it and proceed to prick me with the stinger in the area of my body which felt stagnant or blocked. Interestingly enough, it didn't hurt when he *stung* me with the bee. At times, there was a burning sensation, but most of the time, I felt a vibratory sensation in the area, then it would stop. No swelling, no red marks, nothing. He then gave me the bees who gave of themselves to help heal me. I buried them once I got home.

Being a Licensed Massage Therapist, I also took a slew of classes that not only provided me with continuing education classes but also helped propel my journey into healing as well. It never ceased to amaze me when the right class would be available at the time I was tackling or diving deeper into an aspect I was struggling with. Whether it was physical or mental. All of the classes I took helped me discover the person I am and meant to be. It is a continuous growth.

The spiritual healing came as I took the variety of classes or seminars I attended through the years. God, or should I say the creator as I like to refer to him, had a very bumpy relationship with me. I feared him. I grew up French Catholic, and for whatever reason, my perception as a child was we were terrible and no matter what we did, we would go to hell. It didn't help either that I was angry with him for what happened to me. How could a being who I was told loved me; allow me to endure what I had gone through with no one to turn to. I also was terrified because I still couldn't get the image of Jesus with the thorn cross bleeding out of my head. I can thank Dr. Bruce Lipton, Greg Braden and Dr. Joe Dispenza for helping me change my perception. I was on a work scholarship program with a company called Celebrate Your Life. Working for them enabled me to attend their seminars where I learned most of what we think is just a belief system, which is what we were taught in our upbringing through our various relationships and experiences with the people in our life, from our parents, school, work, religious institution, among many others. This concept allowed me to understand we can heal ourselves just by shifting our power of thought alone. We are energetic beings living a three-dimensional human experience.

This was invaluable information as it allowed me to figure out the third purpose in my life. Which is to live the best version of myself in this lifetime. The way I see it is this way. As I continue to grow and strive to learn the lesson I set out for myself in this amazing adventure we call life, the more marvelous it'll be for everyone and anyone I encounter. Whether they are family, friends, acquaintances or strangers. Why, you may wonder? Because as I shift and change, the people surrounding me may just feel a shift and change in themselves.

I have gone through my healing and growth. I've learned along the way I alone am responsible for it. Yes, I've had help along the way from many various, outstanding practitioners and some outlandish out-of-the-box techniques and modalities. Yet, the biggest part of it all; it was my *choice*. I had one of two *choices* to make. One, sit back, dwell in misery and negativity, complaining about every ache and pain. How life was unfair. How I was always in pain, *or* I could choose to tackle, lean and dive deeper into all that was set forth as a challenge or obstacle in front of me.

At times, I decided to take the road less traveled, certainly feeling the bumps, getting scrapes and bruises along the way. Yet it still got me to where I needed to be. It propelled my journey to discover we all have choices to make in this world. There is no good or bad, right or wrong. Just choices and depending on which one we make, it determines part of the path we are on. Ultimately helping us gain the knowledge of self-discovery and self-awareness in achieving higher enlightenment of who we are as a being. As well as what type of being we wish and choose to be.

My passion in life is fairly simple. To be the best version of myself and to help others discover their best version. How we get there depends solely on their choice and their path. I am simply there to help guide them should they ask me to. It's why I purposely went through this journey we call life.

CHAPTER Thirteen

Midlife Motivation: Relighting an Extinguished Fire
By Janet Zavala

Janet Zavala is a 3-time bestselling author, mid-life mentor, and transformational life coach. Janet specializes in empowering midlife women to thrive in the second act of their lives by helping them navigate life's transitions, discover their true potential, and create a life they love.

Janet is a 30-year corporate employee who followed her passions to create her own reinvention by becoming a successful spiritual practitioner and holistic mentor.

She is the bestselling author of *The Nature of Transformation. A comprehensive life coaching system inspired by nature to heal your mind body and spirit.*

She is a contributing writer to the bestselling books: *Own Your Awesome and Step Into Your Authenticity* and *Be Bold. You Were Never Meant to Fit In.*

She led her organization's Women's Empowerment resource group for five years and is the creator of dynamic programs and workshops that has transformed hundreds of lives.

https://www.janetzavalacoaching.com/

Chapter 13

Midlife Motivation: Relighting an Extinguished Fire

By Janet Zavala

My midlife catastrophe (calling it a crisis doesn't feel adequate) was hitting its apex just as the world was shutting down from a global pandemic. My internal fire in the form of energy, passion, and purpose had been stomped out. My entire life, from my home, body, personal life, to my career were in stages of complete chaos or total destruction. I was at the point of total surrender. When the fire is gone, it's hard to remember if and when it was ever lit. I began to write as a means to reflect and heal while hoping to find and recapture the fire.

I remembered the first time I felt the warmth inside. My desire for adventure lit the fire in my belly to drive cross country at 19 to escape the few opportunities I could see for myself in rural middle America. The fire was kept alive by my survival instincts and a strong craving for the validation I never received as a child. It kept me searching for praise, recognition, and a mythical brass ring of success you occasionally achieve in your professional life. It provided the fuel I needed to keep running from the ghosts of my childhood traumas while running into creative new versions of them in my adult life. The fire felt uncontrollable, as it often can in your twenties. Too much drinking, unhealthy relationships, family discord, and toxic work environments had the potential to engulf and destroy me. The fire burns hot. It can burn your flesh but the dysfunctional warmth is familiar and makes you feel alive. The fun can be deceptive.

I settled down, but did not completely heal, as my twenties came to a close. I found moments of power. I left a toxic company and stepped into another where throughout my thirties I learned to tame my fire by stepping more confidently into my potential at work. I gained momentum with promotions, an intoxicating corporate love-bombing. It made me feel special, giving me the validation (or kindling), I craved.

I thrived and found my passion by becoming one of only a few certified coaches. I led a women's empowerment group, providing coaching and creating workshops. What began to surface was a spark of what could be outside of the comfort of the corporate world. My thirties and forties were about allowing myself to dream about what I wanted to do, not only what I thought I was supposed to do.

I couldn't nurture that fire effectively because I found myself in a trifecta of a midlife crisis: an empty nest, marriage ending, and professional burnout. Sprinkle in feeling the effects of childhood trauma I had successfully avoided for decades and the glories of menopause dawning, and I was on the verge of the breakdown that precedes the catastrophe. Before the fire goes out, there's an explosion, a burning away, of what is no longer essential. My life and career were blowing up. All the things I thought were important to me were falling away.

When the fire went out, I was left with no energy for my passions. What remained was a longing, an ache that resided deep in my soul. I had deep remembrance of what I was capable of and glimmers of the dreams I had, even in the absence of the confidence and motivation that had been stripped away by burnout on the job and the pandemic. I was in search of a second act that had more meaning and less artifice. I didn't know how to get up to make it happen. Months passed. A voice kept calling me to write. Little by little, sentence by sentence, I wrote to heal myself. And in the process, the fire was lit again.

Journal Prompt: We all experience profound personal growth throughout the decades of our lives. There are often commonalities based on the phase of life we experience in our twenties, thirties, forties and so on. Our paths are influenced by the life we were born into and the childhood experiences we had. For each of the decades of your life, journal about your greatest challenges. What did you learn and take with you into the next phase of your life? What did you gladly leave behind? What did you accomplish that you're still proud of to this day? What people in your life do you have the fondest memories of? As you think about the decade that's to come, what do you hope for? What would you like to manifest and bring to life? What does your inner voice keep calling you to do?

As a midlife mentor and coach, I've worked with countless women trying to ignite that fire within. I have not come across one woman in this stage of their life (or approaching this stage) who hasn't expressed this midlife unease. She is at a crossroads where she has been solely focused on meeting family or societal expectations. She is starting to remember the aspirations she had for herself that are unmet. Whether it is taking a chance on a dream that she always had or exploring activities that provide more meaning, she feels compelled to act.

When this feeling is overwhelming, there are typically three responses women have. The first option is to destroy their lives in a desperate search to create the life they crave. Often, the repercussions aren't considered. The desperation has them making decisions that will inevitably wreak havoc on their current situation. It's a time, that if they are struggling with destructive behaviors like addiction, they tend to take a greater hold. Unfortunately, this was the path my mother took when I was nine years old. She was desperate to leave her unfulfilling marriage and had few options, as so many women in the 1970s realized when confronted with this midlife milestone. She blew up her marriage with an affair, shattered the relationship with her children, and eventually sought solace with her emotionally abusive mother. As an adult, I can understand the ache that she had at the time, when the next day seems unbearable and options appear limited. I can't blame her for not making a different choice. Many women were (and many still are) economically imprisoned with limited options. It was also a time when people did not recognize the impact of the traumas they experienced. Although access to information and support has increased, it takes courage to tackle our individual scars and how they are impacting our ability to live the life we want to live.

If you find yourself in a situation where you are desperate to make a change, start planning the next phase of your life. Get clear on what it is you desire. Get the support services you may need in the form of therapy or coaching. Define how you want the next stage of your life to transpire. Take one small action each day that moves you forward into the life that you desire. Trust me, small steps taken consistently over time bring results.

The other option a midlife woman has when she feels the weight of the desire to transform her life into one that she truly wants to live is to essentially give up. When the mountain to your best life feels insurmountable, she resigns herself to live a life that may be comfortable but unfulfilling. It can be a daunting challenge to figure out what it is you want to do next when you have no idea. When speaking to my clients, their biggest anguish is the space between longing for the future that will give them more meaning and the complete confusion over what that ideal future looks like.

Just the simple question of asking yourself, "What's next?" "What am I capable of?" and "What are my aspirations?" can be scary. Looking at a blank page can be intimidating enough for you to close the book completely and put the idea of your ideal future in the dark corner of your bookshelf.

So instead of tackling these very real obstacles, someone decides to resign themselves to a life that may be a little boring, perhaps even a bit toxic because the pain that we know is safer than the uncertainty of an adventure we're not sure we're ready for.

If this option sounds like one that you're considering, you need inspiration. Find people, books, podcasts, videos or any other source to find stories about people who have taken their lives from ordinary to extraordinary. Do activities that you find inspiring like spending time in nature, creative or artistic projects, explore new and interesting hobbies. Expose yourself to new and diverse experiences. Find new ideas about what is possible. You have the power and ability to make this life you're living one that you love.

The final (and best) choice is to explore your heart's desire. This option takes time, attention, and intention, but is the most fun. Approach it with a curious heart and mind. One of the things midlife women are concerned about is time. At this age, we are fully aware of the passage of time. We have more years behind us than in front of us. It's a cruel reality that as soon as we get our shit together and have a little bit more time, time seems to be the thing that we don't have enough of. The desire to choose "right" for that next chapter is palpable. I want to assure you there is no right or wrong choice. There is no wrong path. The only mistake is not choosing a path to explore.

This is the path where you follow your desire and intuition. When you do that, you are going in the right direction. One choice, one action, one activity leads to the next. And the next. And so on. Define the future outcome you desire with as much detail as possible. And then, detach from it. Creating a future vision will lead you down the path you're supposed to travel. Emotionally detaching from the outcome will ensure that you are focused on enjoying the experience and will allow you to be open to the magical changes that will happen along the way.

Exploring your heart's desire starts with maintaining and caring for your overall wellness. The focus on our mental, physical and spiritual health needs to be a priority. Make sure to incorporate plenty of rest. Clearly, this advice is for all that you do in midlife; however, you have work to do to create the life you desire in this second act—whether those activities are in the area of recreation or work. You need a vibrant vessel to do that.

Unapologetically follow your intuition, passions, and desires. These hits of inspiration are no accident. They will lead you down the path you were meant to follow. Along the path, you're exposed to new experiences, people, and places that will advance your learning and enhance your experience.

Trust the process and timing of the universe. It's easy to become impatient. Enjoy every step of the process—the gifts, learning, and people you meet. These are the rewards. It's not too late to begin anything. Your lived experience is meeting your new adventures at just the right time.

If you are preparing for your midlife journey or it is on the horizon, here are a few tips to help you make it through unscathed.

Do Trauma Healing Work. It's time. If you're carrying around the burdens from childhood, unhealed wounds, or unaddressed trauma, as you're nearing midlife (or in midlife), it's time to work through the effects that linger with you. You don't need to carry the weight of those wounds any longer. You've earned some relief.

Strengthen Relationships. The midlife stage is a significant time of evolution for every woman. As you begin to evolve, the people around you may be confused. It can be intimidating when someone close to you begins to break free from the mold. There is an unspoken agreement around people's persona and position in the relationship. We fall into patterns of engagement. When the patterns start to fracture, people get scared.

Your awakening may activate someone else's insecurities.

This is an amazing time to strengthen your relationships by deepening your soul connection. Human evolution is required of all of us. None of us stay the same. When you can evolve with someone who accepts you authentically, you've hit the jackpot of life. Approach those relationships with integrity and honesty. It's one of the hardest things to do—to expose your true self to someone with the hopes of being fully seen. Be that person for someone else. You'll get it in return.

Don't Let Guilt Rob You. We've built a life we love. We have things and experiences created with intention. We enjoy the spoils of our hard work. We may have the thought: "I have so much; how could I want something more?" We begin to feel a little guilty. What's missing is not tangible. It's a longing in our soul. It's our spirit calling for us to follow our intuition more acutely versus following our survival instincts solely. We had to survive. We needed to create security. But now, in midlife, we have the desire that resides deep within us for more significance.

The "M" word. Real talk. Menopause is a son of a bitch. When she arrives, she comes in and makes herself comfortable for far too long. She moves in, unpacks her baggage, and puts her toothbrush in the holder. You're accustomed to her because she has been staying the weekend for a year or two but was called by her fancy name, "perimenopause." She was a well-behaved (if slightly annoying) house guest before. Now she's the roommate from hell that you can't evict. It is incredibly ironic that she shows up just about the time when other parts of your life are falling apart: kids leaving, marriages ending, real sicknesses emerging, the bloom falling off the carefully crafted career. Physical and hormonal challenges sprinkled with the desire for more meaning, and it's no wonder why we need extra compassion for ourselves during this turbulent time. Practice radical self-care and self-compassion. Create routines and rituals around wellness. Consider menopause the "time of you." Seek the treatment and support you need.

Use the Strength and Wisdom You've Earned. We are our worse critics. A client excitedly told me of a big accomplishment she'd been working towards. In the same sentence, she listed three ways in which she "failed," moderating her success with irrelevant insults. We rattle off detailed lists of our flaws while so easily forgetting to celebrate our wins. When asked about our strengths, we answer apologetically and with half-truths. We apologize for our opinions and soften our decisions. Most women have a difficult time recognizing their strengths. The question most of my clients are challenged with is the one where I ask them to tell me what they're good at. Your success is determined by your ability to lean into your strengths. You will stand out and stand apart from the crowd based on what you excel at. Your gifts are no mistake. Claim them proudly.

My passion is to help women stand in their strength and be empowered to use their voices and talents unrestricted. Practice reciting your skills and strengths. Start in the privacy of your bathroom mirror. It's going to feel weird. I know. Be mindful of the language that you use about yourself. Don't minimize your skills and do not criticize yourself. The language you use when referring to yourself gives the person you're speaking with an indication of how to treat you or the opportunities to give you. Only speak of yourself in the highest regard.

Create the Fire for Your Future. Igniting the fire to your second act means that you are designing your life with intention. Create a vision for your life in five years that has no limits. Nearly anything can be achieved in five years' time. Creating a vision trains your brain for action. It keeps the fire going when life and circumstances want to extinguish it.

Your vision can be anything from a professional accomplishment to traveling to 50 countries in five years. Your vision can be about relationships, finances, or any category of life that is most important to the quality of your life at this moment. It should be aspirational. It is likely something you've dreamt about doing or becoming. Tap into your intuition.

If you are struggling, try these journal prompts:

What have been some of your greatest past accomplishments?

Make a list of your skills, abilities, and strengths.

What do you love about yourself?

What have been your most important life lessons?

What are you passionate about?

What activities do you love doing most?

What are your most important values at this stage of your life?

Creating a vision puts you on a path of action. Your vision can change. I would argue, your vision should change as you learn and grow. Your vision is not set in stone. Don't worry about "getting it right." It can be changed as often as you need it to. It's your life. You get to decide.

Welcome to midlife. It can be a seriously confusing and complicated time. It doesn't have to be unfulfilling and tortuous if we settle into the natural occurrence of all of the strange, challenging, and wonderful things that are happening to us. I've never felt more motivated and driven in my life. I'm also acutely aware of when I need to rest, and I give myself downtime without guilt. In fact, guilt has been completely eradicated from my life. My emotional and mental health has reached equal levels with my intellectual capabilities. This means that I have sufficiently healed some of the traumas in my life where I am not derating the strength and wisdom that I possess. I also realize that I'm a work in progress. I have the courage to keep looking at my traumas and triggers in the eyes. I won't let them get the best of me and stop me from living the life I desire. The judgment and criticism I so ruthlessly placed on others and most egregiously on myself has dissipated, making way for higher levels of compassion and empathy.

This chapter is a primer to a book that Janet will release in 2024 to help women navigate and thrive through the unique challenges faced in midlife.

www.ingramcontent.com/pod-product-compliance
Lightning Source LLC
Chambersburg PA
CBHW071312110426
42743CB00042B/1318